THE COMPLETE GUIDE TO MAINE COONS

Jordan Honeycutt

Publication Data

Jordan Honeycutt

The Complete Guide to Maine Coons – First edition.

Summary: "Successfully raising a Main Coon cat from kitten to old age" – Provided by publisher.

ISBN: 978-1-954288-50-8

[1. Main Coons – Non-Fiction] I. Title.

Design by Sorin Rădulescu
First paperback edition, 2022

TABLE OF CONTENTS

CHAPTER 1
What is a Maine Coon Cat?

Physical Characteristics

The Maine Coon cat is one of the largest of all the domesticated cat breeds and has a commanding presence with its large-boned body and full coat. It can be so large, in fact, that it is commonly mistaken for similar-sized wild cats, such as the lynx or bobcat! The Maine Coon can grow to a whopping 40 inches long, stands anywhere from 10–16 inches tall, and typically weighs between 8–18 pounds.

The Maine Coon cat has a long or medium-haired coat that is longer on the flanks and stomach and shorter on the shoulders. Silky and soft in texture, the coat should be heavy and fall smoothly. According to the Cat

Photo Courtesy of Douglas Grenville

Fancier's Association (CFA), the ears should be tufted, wide at the base, and taper to a point. The head should be square and slightly longer in length than width.

The eyes are oval in shape, set wide, and should be expressive. The tail should be wider at the base and taper in length with a long, flowing coat. The cat's body should be muscular and broad, keeping proportion with the rest of the body so that nothing looks exaggerated.

DID YOU KNOW?
World's Heaviest Cat

A Maine Coon cat from New York named Samson is the self-proclaimed largest cat in the city, weighing 28 pounds. Maine Coons typically weigh between 15 and 25 pounds, making them one of the largest cat breeds. Samson's owner, Jonathan Zurbel, says that people often mistake his furry companion for a bobcat because of his size.

2

Maine Coon Cat Colors:

The Maine Coon cat produces a wide variety of accepted colors. They are as follows:

SOLID WHITE – This coat is solid and pure white with a pink nose and pink paw pads. Eyes may be blue when the coat is white.

SOLID BLACK – This is a solid black coat with no red or silver. Paw pads should be black or brown, and the nose should be black.

SOLID CREAM – This coat presents as a solid color with no variations in tone. Paw pads and nose should be pink with the cream coat.

SOLID RED – This coat is a deep red color with no variations, markings, or ticking. Lips, nose, and paw pads should be red in color.

SOLID BLUE – This coat color produces a blue-gray tone throughout with blue-gray paw pads.

BI-COLOR OPTIONS – Bi-color coats come in blue and white, black and white, red and white, and cream and white. Each of these colors ideally presents with white on the bib, belly, and paws.

Parti-Color and White Coats:

TORTOISESHELL – This coat presents as black with one or several shades of red throughout.

BLUE-CREAM – This coat is blue with cream dispersed throughout.

CALICO AND DILUTE CALICO – This coat is white with patches of black and red or white with patches of blue and cream. Mostly white.

These are only a few of the 75 acceptable coat colors and markings. According to the CFA, "any other color with the exception of those showing hybridization resulting in the colors chocolate, lavender, the Himalayan pattern; or these combinations with white [is acceptable.]"

Temperament and Behavior

The Maine Coon cat is a cherished house cat, loved by families all over North America. Known as "gentle giants," this breed has been charming its way across America for decades. The Maine Coon is a highly intelligent cat that is loyal and affectionate toward family but can be cautious and wary of strangers. Though they possess a friendly disposition, they are not typically clingy and appreciate their independence.

Male Maine Coon cats are said to be the more playful of the two sexes, with the females displaying a more dignified presence; however, both genders are equally as gentle and loving. These large cats are typically confident and comfortable around other animals such as dogs and also children.

The Main Coon is also known for its affinity for vocalization. These cats can often be heard yowling, chirping, trilling, and otherwise making vocalizations that sound as if they are carrying on a conversation. While you may think a cat's meow is fairly quiet in nature, these vocalizations can actually be quite loud.

BREED ASSOCIATION
The Maine Coon Cat Club

Established in 1985, the U.K.-based Maine Coon Cat Club is open to everyone, regardless of cat ownership. In addition, the club hosts an annual cat show for local members and produces a yearly wall calendar featuring photos of Maine Coon cats from their members. For more information about the club, visit www.maine-coon-cat-club.com.

These cats are affectionately known as the dogs of the cat world. In fact, Maine Coons can often be seen in the arms of children, being toted around the house with absolutely no qualms. The Maine Coon definitely wins the most patient cat award!

> 66
>
> *Maine Coons are nicknamed the 'dogs of the cat world' and 'gentle giants' for a reason. They are playful, intelligent, and social cats. This makes them ideal companions for people that like to interact with their pets and for families with kids. Maine Coons are often very attached to their owners and will follow them from room to room because of their loyal and curious nature. Most Maine Coons will stay playful, even when older, and require time and attention. They are also very flexible and trainable and are known to enjoy going for walks on a leash. This breed is best suited for people that like spending quality time with their cats.*
>
> JASMINA WALTZ
> *Star-Studded Maine Coons*
>
>

Reaching Full Maturity

> *The Maine Coon breed is by its very nature well-natured; however, Maine Coons, when properly socialized by an experienced breeder, can become adaptable to just about every type of home setting and lifestyle a typical family experiences, from truck drivers taking their Maine Coons on the road (we have a few) to full-time RVers and typical families with children and pets.*
>
> STEVE LANE
> *Florida Maine Coons, LLC*

Maine Coon cats mature more slowly than your average cat breed. They do not hit puberty until the age of one and continue growing to maturity. Most Maine Coons will be mostly grown by the age of eighteen months; however, they do not fully stop growing until somewhere between the ages three and five. These cats maintain their playful, kitten-like nature for several years.

While some Maine Coon cats will exceed expectations and grow to an extremely large size, don't let breeders and Maine Coon fanatics fool you. Many are only slightly larger than their smaller tabby cat counterparts.

Pros and Cons of the Maine Coon Cat

> *The most significant difference between the Maine Coon breed and others is their human-like, soulful nature. The best home will provide a nurturing, loving environment with a true human factor. Just think of the Maine Coon cat as your best friend with a soul.*
>
> GALINA DONOVAN
> *Bellatrix MCO*

*Photo Courtesy
of Victoria Wassell*

Maine Coon cats are delightful feline companions. They love to be touched and held, and they won't leave your side, even in the bathroom.

While we don't believe there are any true "cons" to owning a Maine Coon cat, there are a few aspects of ownership that may be a hindrance. For one, the Maine Coon is a very vocal cat, as discussed above, and can carry on conversations during the most inconvenient times. This may be in the middle of the night or during an important phone call for work.

The Maine Coon also sheds like any other domesticated cat. The longer, fluffy coat can shed year-round or seasonally, depending on climate and individual genetics. The Maine Coon also has an un-catlike love of water and can often be seen digging in their water bowl and as a result, tipping it over. Many Maine Coon owners will place the water bowl in a bathtub so that they aren't cleaning up puddles every time their cats get the urge to make a mess.

One final con of the Maine Coon cat is the cost to own one. While you can pick up any house cat at a local shelter for a small expense, a purebred Maine Coon cat will cost you anywhere from $2500-$6000.

Keep in mind that while the upfront purchase price may be a one-time expense, caring for any pet, even a Maine Coon cat, will cost money each year. From spaying and neutering, to annual check-ups, medications, and daily maintenance such as food and scratching posts, the cost can be significant. Make sure you are able to properly care for your Maine Coon before making the decision to purchase one.

History of the Maine Coon Cat

The origins of the Maine Coon cat are unclear. It is thought they originated in America, as there is no record of them elsewhere around the world; however, it is unknown how the breed began.

Maine Coon Cat Folklore

While their history remains a mystery, there are many myths that have circulated over the years that have attempted to explain the breed, including the mysterious nature and size of these beautiful creatures. The first is that they are somehow related to raccoons. Though this has now been deemed scientifically impossible, many people used to believe that Maine Coons' large-sized, bushy tails and sometimes raccoon-like markings were a direct result of cross-species breeding.

Another myth popular among cat fanatics is the cats' potential royal origin. It is rumored that Marie Antoinette planned to flee France and had placed six long-haired Angora cats on a ship to make the journey to America ahead of her. Though she did not make it safely, her beloved cats did and soon began mating with the domestic short-haired cats in Maine.

FAMOUS MAINE COONS!
Cosey the Cat

In 1895, the first North American cat show was hosted in New York City, where a Maine Coon cat named Cosey won the silver collar and medallion and was named "Best Long-haired Cat in Show." Cosey was owned by Mrs. Fred Brown and was born in 1893. Cosey's silver collar and medallion are now owned by the Cat Fancier's Association (CFA) and housed at their central office.

*Photo Courtesy
of Ahli Stevens*

The most probable theory is that the ships traveling to America took several long-haired Angora cats along to control the pest population on the ships. These cats most likely began breeding with the native short-haired cats, producing what we now know as the Maine Coon.

Troubled Past

Regardless of how the breed began, their fate was soon troubled. When the first North American cat show was hosted in 1895 in Madison Square Garden, a female Maine Coon brown tabby, Cosey, was named best in show. After this moment of fame, though, the breed made a sharp decline in popularity. In fact, the Maine Coon was even declared extinct by some in the 1950s. This was partially due to an influx of other long-haired cat breeds to America, including Persian cats.

It wasn't until the 1950s, when Ethylin Whittemore, Alta Smith, and Ruby Dyer created the Central Maine Cat Club, that the breed began to come back into the hearts of Americans. Within this club, the first breed standards for the Maine Coon originated.

The Return of the Maine Coon Cat

After the breed was finally given official breed status in 1976 by the CFA, the cats began to reenter the show ring, catching the eye of people once more. Eventually, their newfound popularity led Maine officially to declare the Maine Coon its state cat. As of 2021, the Maine Coon cat remains the third most popular cat breed in America.

The Tale of a Clone

Maine Coon cats are so beloved by their owners that some even wish to have their feline companions cloned. In fact, the first commercially cloned cat was a cloned version of a 17-year- old Maine Coon named Nicky. Little Nicky, as the clone was called, was

DID YOU KNOW?
Official State Cat

The Maine Coon cat was recognized as the official state cat of Maine in 1985. Maine Coons are considered one of the oldest natural breeds in North America, being a native to the state. Their large, rounded feet allow them to walk quietly through the soft snow during winter in the forests of Maine.

produced in 2004 after a woman in North Texas paid $50,000 to recreate her deceased pet.

While the original Nicky had no health issues during his life, Little Nicky was plagued with issues his predecessor did not have. While there is no proof this was due to the cloning process, that is one speculation. The owner claimed that Little Nicky possessed a similar personality and physical traits to the original Nicky.

CHAPTER 2

Finding a Maine Coon Cat

> "
>
> *The Maine Coon is a congenial and flexible breed of cat. They can thrive in a wide variety of family/people environments, as long as they are with people who prefer interactive pets. Maine Coons really like people and want to be with their owners as much as possible, often following them from room to room and inserting themselves into whatever process or activity their people are doing. Conversely, they will not do well in an environment where they are left entirely alone by their owners for long work days, particularly if those days are compounded by long evenings where the owner is away from the house again. If they do not have other four-footed buddies, Maine Coons in this situation may become skittish and retiring or may be excessively needy with their people when they are at home. The other point to consider is that Maine Coons get to be large cats with long legs and tails, and homes with lots of precious breakable objects are not the best fit. In general, Maine Coons adapt well to other household pets, particularly when they are introduced as kittens.*
>
> TERI MATZKIN
> *SaraJen Maine Coon Cats*
>
> "

Once you decide a Maine Coon cat is right for you, you may be ready to start the search for a kitten. Before you reach out to the first breeder or shelter you find, there are several things you need to understand about the process. This chapter will dive into the details about buying from a breeder versus adopting and how to determine which decision is best for you.

Buying vs. Adopting

When looking for a Maine Coon cat, there are two general ways to do it. You can adopt a kitten or an older Maine Coon from a rescue center, or you can purchase a Maine Coon kitten from a reputable breeder. Though many are strong proponents of adoption, there is no right or wrong when it comes to choosing your feline companion.

Adopting a kitten or adult cat that needs a home is an honorable thing to do, but there are some difficult aspects of cat adoption. First, if you wish to adopt a pure-bred Maine Coon, you will have a very difficult time finding one at a local shelter, so you will need to seek a Maine Coon specific rescue center. It is possible to find a Maine Coon cross in a shelter. However, a shelter cat's genetic origin is never certain, so you likely won't ever know for sure if he possesses Maine Coon genetics unless you do DNA testing.

Photo Courtesy
of Liz Holmes
Monster Maine Coons

Aside from unknown genetic makeup, an adult cat in a shelter has an unknown past and could potentially struggle with human companionship. No matter how gentle and friendly a breed like the Maine Coon is, trauma, abuse, and neglect can all affect a cat's personality and the way he interacts with his human or animal family. If you do not feel capable or equipped to handle a cat with previous trauma, you may want to rethink adopting an older cat from a rescue center or shelter. If you do choose to adopt, be sure you are aware of any issues ahead of time. Adopt a well-adjusted Maine Coon or choose to buy one from a breeder instead.

Just because a cat is in a shelter doesn't mean he will struggle with past traumas or be difficult to get along with; however, it is something to be aware of before you bring him home. An adult cat in a shelter is more likely to be dealing with fear or feelings of abandonment than a young kitten that hasn't known another life. On the other hand, you will be able to better judge a mature cat's personality and individual temperament better than you would a kitten. For example, if a particular Maine Coon doesn't do well with children, that is something the shelter should know and tell you before you bring him home to a house full of kids.

As we've discussed, there are both pros and cons to adopting a rescue Maine Coon cat, so do your due diligence on each animal and facility before deciding which route to take to bring your Maine Coon home with you.

Rescues and Shelters 101

> "
>
> *With a rescue, you will get mixed lines. The likelihood of a purebred Maine Coon being in a rescue is incredibly low, as these are expensive felines to import and export. Adopt before you shop is what I say (even on my own website), but if you are going to shop, make sure you focus on facts and proof. Don't let that cute fuzzy kitten pull on your heartstrings.*
>
> KOSMOS L KNOVAS
> *KosmikCattery LLC*
>
> "

If you decide to adopt a Maine Coon, you need to know where to look and how these facilities operate. In the United States, there are three different classifications for pet and animal rescues: municipal shelters, no-kill shelters, and nonprofit rescue organizations. Below is a brief description of each.

MUNICIPAL SHELTERS: These shelters take in strays, abandoned animals, and animals surrendered by their owners. They are operated and funded by local governments. The animals there have a limited time to be adopted and are often euthanized due to a lack of space for new intakes.

Adoption fees are typically low at these places. Almost all require an animal to be spayed or neutered before it is adopted. The cats are housed in kennels and are maintained with basic veterinary care while they remain in the shelter.

If you adopt from a shelter, be aware that the stressful environment can cause a cat to act aloof, fearful, or even aggressive, even if that is not the animal's true personality.

NO-KILL SHELTERS: These are private organizations that will not kill a healthy and adoptable cat. Because they do not euthanize animals, they have a limited intake policy and end up turning many animals away due to lack of space.

Cats are often kept in no-kill shelters for an extended time; months and sometimes even years go by before they are adopted. If a facility is full, foster homes are often used. Many times, this can help avoid "kennel syndrome" and help a traumatized Maine Coon adjust and become more adoptable.

NON-PROFIT RESCUE ORGANIZATIONS: These organizations are mostly run and operated by volunteers. They utilize foster houses to save as many animals as possible. They do not euthanize animals.

These organizations are typically privately funded or donation dependent. Many rescues are breed-specific and, as such, are dedicated to rescuing one breed, such as the Maine Coon. Rescues offer the same basic

*Photo Courtesy
of Diane Ingvarsson*

veterinarian care as municipal shelters but often have to pay face-value prices, leading to higher adoption fees.

Most rescue groups rely heavily on foster families. Some may not have a physical facility at all but instead maintain a website with information about their available cats. Because the cat lives with a foster family, more is known about the cat's personality, making it easier to find the animal a compatible home.

HELPFUL TIP
Specialty Purebred Cat Rescue

For prospective cat owners looking for adoptable Maine Coon cats, Specialty Purebred Cat Rescue is a good resource. This foster-based rescue is based out of the Midwest and is a 501(C)3 nonprofit. Maine Coons are one of the many breeds rescued by this organization. All available cats are viewable on their website at www.purebredcatrescue.org.

Rescue organizations typically have much stricter adoption guidelines and policies, frequently requiring a home inspection before approval. Much like with a typical breeder, many have policies in place that require adopters to return the cat to the rescue if they can no longer keep the animal. You are much more likely to find a pure-bred Maine Coon cat at a breed-specific rescue center than a municipal shelter or a no-kill shelter.

Tips for Adoption

When adopting a Maine Coon from a rescue center, there are a few things you can do to help ease the stress of the search. While it's unlikely you will find a Maine Coon at a local municipal shelter, don't hesitate to call anyway and let them know exactly what you're looking for. Ask them to be on the lookout for a Maine Coon cat or a possible Maine Coon cross and to give you a call if one comes in. If you have any specific parameters, tell them those as well, but remember, the more specific you are, the longer it may take to find the cat you're looking for.

Rescue animals, even cats, often show a special appreciation for a chance at a forever home and a family to call their own. If you're planning to contact a Maine Coon specific rescue, know that they often have applications and screening processes. Get your information in quickly if you find a Maine Coon you love. It's not uncommon for these breed-specific rescue centers to have a lengthy waitlist.

CHAPTER 3
All About Maine Coon Breeders

If you decide a breeder is the right route for you and your family to find a Maine Coon cat companion, be sure you're looking at reputable ones. Beware of backyard breeders who breed animals for the sole purpose of making a profit while often neglecting the care of the breed and the animals in their facility. These places are a breeding ground for genetic diseases and other illnesses.

Finding a Breeder

> *When choosing a breeder, it's important to make sure that they are registered with a cat association and provide registration paperwork for your kitten or cat. The two big registries in the US are TICA and CFA. Registration paperwork is not expensive for the breeder and ensures that the cat truly is a Maine Coon. The next step is making sure that the breeder does health testing, since Maine Coons have a higher rate of HCM (hypertrophic cardiomyopathy, a heart disease) and hip dysplasia. Testing should consist of DNA testing, yearly heart echocardiograms, and hip X-rays for every breeding cat. The cats should also be tested and negative for FIV/FeLV.*
>
> *Preferable are catteries that let you visit, to make sure the cats look healthy, have enough space, adequate entertainment, and a clean environment. A good breeder will ask a lot of questions about you and will welcome questions from you.*
>
> JASMINA WALTZ
> *Star-Studded Maine Coons*

A great place to begin your Maine Coon breeder search is by word of mouth. Do you have friends or family that have a Maine Coon cat? If so, what breeder did they use? If you don't know anyone with a Maine Coon cat you can ask, try an internet search.

Find a Maine Coon breeder in your area and check reviews on Facebook, Yelp, and Google. These reviews can be very helpful in catching any red flags or irresponsible breeders before it's too late. Remember that reviews often reflect one side of a very personal story, so don't let one negative review turn you away if the majority are positive.

Facebook also has several Maine Coon cat groups that you can join for free. These groups are great for providing personal Maine Coon stories, information, feedback from other owners, and even breeder information. These virtual groups allow you to connect with owners around the world in a way that wasn't possible in previous decades.

Breeder Reputation

"

When choosing a Maine Coon breeder to work with, your focus should be on the overall health, temperament, and well-being of the kittens/cats that the breeder produces and raises. If possible, it is best to visit the breeder before making a final kitten selection to make sure you are comfortable with the breeding conditions, avoiding overcrowded and unclean situations where infectious diseases may be prevalent. It is also important to work with a breeder who does all the appropriate genetic testing available to enhance the sturdiness of their breeding program. If looking for 'real' Maine Coons from a rescue organization, be aware that many so-called Maine Coons advertised are merely longhaired domestic cats that may only have a characteristic or two that resemble those of Maine Coons. These cats still deserve to be rescued and loved, but they may not have the true temperament of the real thing.

TERI MATZKIN
SaraJen Maine Coon Cats

Breeder reputation is one of the most important aspects in your search for a Maine Coon cat. A reputable breeder will meet certain standards that an average "backyard breeder" or cattery will not. A healthy Maine Coon should be your top priority when searching for a breeder, but it can be difficult to determine the good breeders from the bad. Here are some of the key factors and questions to ask to help you determine a quality breeder from one that is not.

Are They Certified?

A reputable and trustworthy cattery will be certified by one of the top registries, such as the CFA, TICA, or the FIFE. Breeders certified under these registries understand the breed standard and are committed to the betterment of the breed first and foremost. Any kitten you purchase from a certified breeder will come with registry papers.

Photo Courtesy of Liz Holmes Monster Maine Coons

Can I Visit the Cattery?

A reputable breeder should welcome a potential adoptee into the cattery. Due to health concerns, they might not allow you into certain areas of the facility because there is a concern of tracking in diseases that could be detrimental to a young kitten's undeveloped immune system. However, a breeder should always allow you to come on-site and see other Maine Coons in the program. If a reputable cattery does not allow visitors, they should send videos and pictures of your kitten and the facility.

BREED ASSOCIATION

United Maine Coon Cat Association (UMCCA)

The United Maine Coon Cat Association (UMCCA) was founded on December 1, 1972, and is the Maine Coon Cat Breed club of the Cat Fancier's Federation (CFF). The UMCCA has four levels of membership: Honorary, Fancier, Associate, and Breeder. A list of UMCCA breeder members can be viewed on the association's website, www.umcca.org.

How Long Have You Been Breeding Maine Coons?

Optimally, you will want to seek out a breeder with many years of experience who has produced many proven healthy litters. A quality breeder with adequate experience will know how to breed only the most desirable traits and healthy Maine Coons.

What Genetic Conditions Do You Test for Before Breeding, and What Conditions Do You Screen the Kittens for Before Selling?

All purebred cats are prone to certain genetic diseases and conditions. These will be discussed in greater detail in chapter 11. Before purchasing, it's highly important to ask for a detailed list of the tests and screens performed on the parents, as well as copies of the test results. Be aware that having a cat "checked out" by a vet is not the same as genetic testing.

Purchasing a Maine Coon from a breeder that does not perform genetic testing on their animals is risky and increases the chance your cat will be affected by common breed-specific genetic conditions such as hypertrophic cardiomyopathy (HCM), spinal muscular atrophy (SMA), hip dysplasia, and more. While genetic testing does not guarantee your cat will be healthy for life, it greatly reduces the chance your cat will have to deal with these costly and heartbreaking diseases.

Can I See Veterinary Records for Both Parents?

Choosing a Maine Coon is a significant investment that will potentially affect your life for the next ten to twenty years. It's very important that the breeder you choose is open and transparent with information regarding the parent cats. If the breeder is not willing to share medical records, you should find another breeder. Both cat parents should have been checked by specialists and cleared for defects. The breeder should also provide proof of genetic testing. Finding a certified Maine Coon breeder should ensure that proper genetic testing is done.

Do You Ever Sell to a Broker or Pet Shop?

If the answer is yes, walk away from this cattery immediately. Kittens found in pet shops are bred for profit alone and come with no health guarantee. A responsible breeder, breeding for the betterment of the Maine Coon breed and the cat's health and appearance, will never sell an animal to a broker or a pet store. Reputable breeders are heavily invested in their cats and will want to meet the families of each of their kittens to be sure they will be properly cared for.

Get it in Writing

> *Always make sure you are communicating with a real breeder or rescue. There are a lot of scammers preying on those who want a Maine Coon. Check with TICA and CFA registries to confirm that the cattery is real. If the price is too good to be true, it's probably a scam. Purebred Maine Coons are rarely priced under $1,000. If the person is pushing you to send money, consider a different breeder. Never buy a kitten from a web page that has a buy-now button; they are scams. Find a breeder that conducts health and DNA tests. You want to make sure the kitten you are getting has healthy genetics. A lot of rescues list longhaired cats as Maine Coons, but it's hard to know if cats are purebred without a DNA test unless the cat was owner-surrendered.*
>
> CORIE AND MATTHEW HELMS
> *Rocketmans Maine Coons*

Along with registration papers, your kitten should come with a contract detailing all the things mentioned above. This contract is more than just proof of purchase. It details all your rights as the buyer and the breeder's rights. This contract should state breeder responsibilities, such as genetic testing, vet records, and proof of lineage, as well as any stipulations such as breeding rights, what should happen to the Maine Coon if you can no longer care for him, and even an age by which your cat must be spayed or neutered.

Maine Coons that come with breeding rights, meaning you may breed your cat to produce offspring, will often come with stipulations. These commonly include not breeding your Maine Coon until he or she reaches a certain age. This helps increase the chances of a healthy litter and also gives the parent cat a chance to show signs of any genetic conditions before. If your cat does show signs of a genetic condition, the contract should mandate spay and neuter and revoke breeding rights, as this is for the betterment of the breed as a whole.

Your breeder contract may also stipulate whether you can or cannot show your Maine Coon in cat shows. If cat shows interest you, ask ahead of time what your rights are in this regard.

Among the basics in a breeder contract, a health guarantee should be included. This health guarantee should ensure your cat does not develop any genetic conditions within a certain time frame, typically two to five years. Look for breeders who will refund all or part of your cat's purchase price if such conditions do arise.

Many breeders will offer a replacement cat, but many owners will decline this offer as they have already bonded and become close to the cat they purchased. This is why a refund should be an option detailed in the breeder contract in the event of genetic conditions.

Be sure to clear up any questions or concerns before signing a contract so that you know exactly what you are spending your money on.

Choosing a Maine Coon Kitten

> "
>
> *Choosing the best Maine Coon depends a lot on the home the cat will be entering. If there are small children or rowdy dogs, which might stress a cat, then choose a brave cat or kitten. In general, though, kittens adjust well to children and animals, and existing pets find the addition of a baby animal (i.e., kittens) nonthreatening, if a bit annoying at times. If bringing an adult Maine Coon into a home with existing pets, first try to find out if the new Maine Coon gets along with other animals or not. A home with no small children and no other pets could probably bring in any Maine Coon cat or kitten and it would adjust.*
>
> CARON JANTZEN
> *Bald Mountain Maine Coons*
>
> "

Once you have found a reputable breeder, you will soon be ready to choose your Maine Coon kitten. Here are a few things to consider and look for when picking out the perfect kitten for you and your family!

Check for Health

At a minimum, before choosing a kitten from a litter, check for basic health. The eyes and nose should be clear, ears should be clean, and the cat should have bright eyes and a healthy coat. The kittens should be moving around with ease and show no signs of discomfort, and their bellies should not be distended.

While the kittens should be playful and energetic, they should not be showing signs of aggression or acting fearful. These are not traits that a reputable Maine Coon breeder will be breeding into a healthy litter.

If you see any kittens in a litter that do not meet these standards, you may want to seek out a different breeder. A healthy litter will not show these signs, and a reputable breeder will not sell kittens that do not meet their health standards.

Male vs. Female

When choosing a gender, it's important to know how each is different. Males, also known as Toms, can be more affectionate and friendly and grow larger, but they can also be territorial and "spray" if they aren't neutered. Intact males will also howl to call out to females and be more likely to roam.

Female Maine Coons are commonly a bit more reserved than their male counterparts but are far less likely to be territorial. Females also howl when they go into heat and can become pregnant at a young age.

Though these guidelines can help you decide between genders, each Maine Coon will have his or her own personality and contribute great love and affection to your family.

One Cat or More?

Despite the common misconception cats are solitary and like to be alone, bringing home two kittens at once is not always a bad idea. In fact, there are several pros to bringing two kittens home at once.

COMPANIONSHIP: Cats may appreciate their alone time and personal space, but a cat left alone for too long can get bored and become destructive. Bringing home two kittens at once ensures that your cats always have a companion and someone to keep them active.

If you attempt to bring home a kitten to an adult cat, your adult cat may have a hard time adjusting and sharing his space. Bringing home two kittens from the same litter can actually make two-cat life easier, as they have already bonded as littermates.

Photo Courtesy
of Liz Holmes
Monster Maine Coons

GROOMING: Having two cats means there is always a kitty companion there to help with grooming. While cats groom themselves pretty efficiently, another cat will help them get those spots that are difficult to reach. Plus, it's just plain cute watching them groom each other!

EXERCISE: Having two kittens means there is always another energetic ball of fluff ready to play. This can be great when you aren't always available to play yourself. Having a kitten companion can provide them with all the exercise they need to stay fit and healthy.

Though there are several pros to bringing home two kittens at once, this doesn't mean you can't purchase just one. One kitten will do well with a family that can provide him with consistent companionship and affection. He or she will likely become "ruler" of the house and provide you with lots of love and laughter for years to come.

CHAPTER 4

Preparing for Your Maine Coon Cat

> "
>
> *When bringing a new Maine Coon kitten into your home, prepare a room or small suite of rooms for the cat to get used to initially. This should be a space where the owner/s can spend time with the kitten, playing with it and handling/petting it. You want the kitten to easily find its litter box and food and start to experience the smells and atmosphere of your home, before being exposed to the entire multi-room, multi-floor house. It's also important for the owner to be able to see if the kitten is eating and using its box appropriately during this time. While the kitten is in this introductory space, be sure to provide some soft music or talk radio/streaming to help it feel less alone and strange. For most Maine Coon kittens, this initial period will only take a few days at most, because they will actually be very eager to explore the adventures outside that space!*
>
> TERI MATZKIN
> *SaraJen Maine Coon Cats*
>
> "

Pick-up day is one of excitement and anticipation as you bring your new loving Maine Coon into your life and your home. While this is definitely a day to look forward to, you must also prepare to bring your Maine Coon home ahead of time to ensure he is coming into a safe environment where he can blossom into the loving cat he has the potential to be.

This chapter will walk you through all you need to know before you bring home your Maine Coon. From preparing other pets to kitten-proofing your home and so much more, you can rest assured you will be prepared and ready when that exciting day comes!

Preparing Other Pets

> *To introduce a Maine Coon kitten (or cat) to other pets, expose the animals to the scent of each other before they actually meet. This is especially important when bringing an adult cat into a home with other pets. (Kittens tend to be less threatening.) So if the new Maine Coon is confined to one room, at some point, remove it from that room and let the other animals enter and have a good sniff. When the animals finally do meet, don't expect love at first sight—or even like at first sight—especially if these are two cats meeting for the first time. There could be some posturing and growling, but as long as the cats don't start fighting, everything should be fine. If bringing a kitten/cat into a home with dog(s), I would let the new Maine Coon investigate the dogs in its own time rather than forcing the introduction. Just make sure the dogs don't chase the new Maine Coon when they finally do meet.*
>
> CARON JANTZEN
> *Bald Mountain Maine Coons*

When you're preparing to bring your new Maine Coon home, make sure you don't neglect to prepare any existing pets. While some cats will do well just thrown together, assuming you can simply let them mix and all will be well may not be the best idea and could result in physical or emotional trauma for both your new Maine Coon and your existing animals.

Whether you're preparing a resident cat, a dog, or even other small animals, they all will need care and time to become acquainted with each other, even before they meet face to face. This will increase the likelihood of a positive and successful relationship going forward.

Preparing a Resident Cat

When you bring your new Maine Coon home to another resident cat, it's important to get them well acquainted even before they meet face to face.

EXCHANGE SCENTS – It's important to introduce your resident cat to your new kitten gradually by first allowing him to become comfortable with the

28

Photo Courtesy of Victoria Wassell

scent of your Maine Coon. Check with the breeder to see if they will allow you to bring home a blanket with your new kitten's scent before pick-up day. You may need to take a clean blanket to the breeder beforehand and then pick it up after a few days with your kitten.

Once you have a blanket or other item with your kitten's scent, introduce it to your resident cat and allow the item to remain in a common area of the house. This probably won't be too off-putting for your cat, and it will acclimate him to the scent of another cat in the home.

SEPARATE SPACES – Before you bring your new Maine Coon home, prepare a separate room for him so he can spend time alone. This may be a bedroom, office, or any other space that can be completely separated from the rest of the house. Alternate this space between your new Maine Coon and your resident cat. This will once again allow them to acclimate to each other's scents without being thrust upon each other too quickly.

Make sure each space has water, litter box access, and plenty of social interaction. This room is just temporary but should still have all the basic necessities for your Maine Coon to thrive. As the cats swap spaces, they will use each other's water dishes, litter boxes, and toys.

Allow your cats to interact through the closed door, as they will probably both be curious about the other feline in the home. You can even feed them near the closed door so they get used to eating near each other.

While doing this exchange, if either cat becomes stressed or scared, continue to keep them separated until the fear and stress is relieved, which typically just takes time. This process may take a few days for some cats or a week or two for others. As long as both cats are calm near each other and seem to be handling the exchanges well, it's time to move on to a visual meeting.

LET THEM SEE EACH OTHER – When you feel your cats are ready to meet, begin with a visual meeting through a glass door or a barrier such as a baby gate. If using a baby gate, stack two if needed to make sure neither cat will jump over the gate. Keep the cats separated but visible to each other and allow them to eat and play that way.

Photo Courtesy of Ahli Stevens

Keep the cats separated for as long as you feel they need it. Once ready, slowly remove the barrier and allow your cats to meet each other fully. Keep a close eye on both your resident cat and your new Maine Coon to make sure things remain calm. A little hissing may occur; however, it should dissipate quickly, and the two should soon interact calmly. If not, separate the cats and continue exchanging spaces and scents, keeping them separate, but in sight of each other, until they become calmer.

If your resident cat is having trouble acclimating to his new companion, understand that this has been his domain up until this point and allow him ample time to adjust. It is certainly not impossible to acclimate another cat into a home with a resident cat, but it can be a challenge and sometimes requires patience and persistence.

How to Prepare Existing Dogs

> *When introducing your Maine Coon to an existing pet, watch your pet for signs of jealousy or indications of being territorial. For example, your existing pet may be the sweetest pet ever but may bite if its food is eaten out of the food bowl by a Maine Coon. Remember, Maine Coons REALLY LOVE FOOD, whether it is your food or another pet's!*
>
> LYNN BARNETT
> *Crescent Moon Maine Coons*

Before you decide to bring home a Maine Coon cat to an existing dog, you should consider your dog's personality and past. If your dog has had any previous run-ins with cats or other small animals in which he chased them or acted at all aggressively, you may want to reconsider. Not all dogs are suited to live in harmony with cats. Only you know your dog, but if you have any doubts or questions, you may want to take your dog out on a leash and see how he interacts with a cat before you attempt bringing home a cat.

If you decide to bring home a Maine Coon cat to an existing dog, follow the same steps listed above when introducing a new Maine Coon to a resident cat. Begin by introducing the scent with a blanket or other item before you bring your cat home, then put him in a separate room before beginning introductions.

Depending on the personality or energy level of your dog, he may get overly excited and whine or scratch at the door where your cat is. This isn't always a sign of aggression; it could just mean your dog is excited to meet his new friend and play. Try to distract him and keep him calm by keeping to his normal routine.

INTRODUCE THEM ON A LEASH – When you feel your dog is ready to meet your cat, do so carefully. Take the two animals to a neutral area they don't normally go to, so there are no territorial issues during the first meeting. Keep your dog leashed and have another person hold your Maine Coon to keep him secure. If you're bringing home a kitten, he will most likely be more than willing to make friends with your dog, but you need to make sure your dog is receptive.

Praise your dog and reaffirm him for good and positive behavior as the first meeting begins. Pay careful attention to your dog's cues during this meeting, and if you notice any signs of distress, aggression, or other negative emotions,

Photo Courtesy
of Douglas Grenville

FUN FACT
Popular Felines

As of 2019, the Maine Coon cat was listed as the fifth most popular cat breed by the CFA. This ranking was determined by the number of cats of each breed registered with the CFA in 2019. Maine Coons were ranked third most popular in 2015 and fifth in 2016, 2017, 2018, and 2019.

separate the two and let them calm down before trying again.

Depending on your dog's reaction, you may need to repeat the leashed introduction several times before the animals are calm and comfortable around each other. Take the time to do so, as rushing into unleashed meetings can be both stressful and dangerous for your cat if the animals are not ready.

UNLEASHED MEETINGS – Once the two animals can remain calm and comfortable around each other, remove the leash from your dog and allow him to greet your cat, which should still be held securely at first. Pet and love on your new cat while simultaneously showing affection to your dog. This will help to show the dog that this is a new member of the family and not a threat. If the interaction is going well, let your cat down to explore your dog and watch a new friendship blossom.

If you are determined to make the relationship work and your animals are struggling to peacefully intermingle, consider hiring an animal behaviorist for help. Do not ever leave your dog and cat unsupervised until your cat is old enough to defend himself and you are certain they are getting along. Make sure your cat always has a space to escape to when needed, preferably a place up high that your dog cannot access.

Other Small Pets and Your Maine Coon

If you have other small pets in your home, such as a bird or a hamster, be sure you prepare their spaces before bringing home your Maine Coon. Cats are predators and will naturally hunt and even kill small animals, so it's important to keep their enclosures fully secure at all times.

Keeping a cat and other small animals in the same home is possible, but precautions should always be in place. Do not attempt to let them interact freely, as instinct may take over for your Maine Coon. If the enclosure is secure, you may allow your cat to view your other small pets, but if your cat is causing your other animals stress, separate them for the sake of your small pets.

Preparing Children and Family

> *When you first bring your kitten or cat home, keep it separated from pets for a few days until the animals are comfortable. It helps to allow the kitten and your other pets to smell each other from under the door. Use the same brush to groom your other pets as you use on the kitten to get the animals used to each other's smell. When you finally allow them into the same room, watch them closely for any aggression. Do not force them to interact. Some hissing and growling from other pet cats is common. Sometimes you can get them to bond by playing with them at the same time or by giving them all treats together. Kittens are easier than adult cats to introduce into a home that already has pets. When introducing your kitten to its new family, limit interactions to only a few people at a time. You do not want to scare and overwhelm the kitten. Do not force the kitten to be held. Have family members take turns playing with the kitten or giving it treats. If your kitten is scared when you start having visitors to your house, have your visitors also try giving your kitten treats or playing with it.*
>
> CORIE AND MATTHEW HELMS
> *Rocketmans Maine Coons*

Existing pets are not the only ones that need to be prepared to meet your new Maine Coon. There are several things you should teach your children and family before that exciting day to keep everyone safe and happy.

HOW TO HOLD A KITTEN – If you are bringing home a Maine Coon kitten from a breeder, it's important that all members of the family know how to properly handle him. Kittens are delicate and can be injured easily, even with a well-intentioned squeeze. Teach your children how to properly handle your kitten and set boundaries before he comes home to prevent trauma and stress.

When picking up your kitten, always support his body and backside. Lift gently with your hand under his belly, holding securely but not too tight. Never pull your kitten by the legs or tail. Though mother cats often transport their kittens by the scruff of their neck, this is not something you should attempt to do as it can cause stress or accidental injury.

While it's important to hold your kitten properly, it is also beneficial to hold him often from a young age. This can help your kitten become accustomed to being handled, which will likely mean he will tolerate being handled well as an adult.

Remind children that cats have claws and to be careful when handling a cat of any age. Long sleeves and gloves may be beneficial for young kids when handling the cat until they are mature enough to handle him without fear of being scratched.

Along with proper handling, it's important to discuss proper boundaries. Teach your kids to leave the cat alone when he displays signs of stress or when he tries to walk away. Forcing a cat to be held when he doesn't want to be interacted with can cause stress and can lead to injury for your cat or children.

Kitten-Proof Your Home

> *In general, bringing a Maine Coon kitten home isn't much different from any other kitten. Young kittens are extremely curious and will do things adult cats might not do, so it's important to make your place kitten-proof. Pick up all little things that shouldn't go into a tiny kitten belly, like small Legos, strings, small toys, etc. Kittens will even chew on cables, but you can find cable covers online to keep them safe. Prevent them from having access to higher places they could fall from. It's also important to only use non-clumping litter for young kittens, since clumping litter can cause a blockage if ingested because kitten stomachs are a lot smaller. All kittens eat a lot, so stock up on food! There is one difference from other cat breeds, mostly concerning male Maine Coons...they do get larger and taller than your average cat, so litter boxes, carriers, cat trees, and beds should be larger too. We often buy products made for medium-sized dogs, so that the cats have enough space.*
>
> JASMINA WALTZ
> *Star-Studded Maine Coons*

Kittens are playful and curious creatures that will get into a can find. This mischief can be downright cute, but it can also po your kitten gets into something he shouldn't. Take the time to kitten-proof your home before pick-up day so that your Maine Coon can stay safe and healthy while in your house.

PUT AWAY CORDS – Just like human babies, kittens explore the world primarily with their mouths. You may not think that a television cord is a threat, but when a curious kitten begins to paw and chew on it, it becomes a danger. Tie up all loose cords in the house so that they are not tempting playthings for your kitten.

If the cords become an issue for your cat, run them through PVC pipe to keep them covered and out of reach. Alternatively, you can spray the cords with a commercial bitter apple spray to help deter him. If your kitten just seems to love chewing, firmly tell him no when he approaches the cords and offer him an acceptable chew toy instead.

CLOSE THE WASHER AND DRYER – While it may not seem obvious, leaving the washer or dryer open can be dangerous for your Maine Coon. Cats are always looking for a cozy spot to hide, and the well of a washer or dryer can be very appealing to your feline friend. This becomes a serious threat when the person doing laundry is unaware the cat is in there. If you must leave the machines open for any reason, close the door and shut your Maine Coon out of the room.

KEEP THE TOILETS SHUT – Toilet lids should remain down all the time so your thirsty kitten doesn't accidentally go for a swim he can't get out of. Don't be fooled into thinking he can't get up that high.

HOUSEPLANTS TO WATCH OUT FOR – Houseplants and cats often do not go well together. Aside from the fact that your cat will likely destroy your houseplants by chewing on them, there are many common varieties that can be toxic to your furry companion.

Some extremely common houseplants that are toxic for cats include pothos, monstera deliciosa, peace lilies, aloe vera, snake plants, English ivy, and dumb cane. If ingested, these plants can cause anything from mild tummy upset to difficulty breathing.

These are not the only common houseplants that pose a threat to your Maine Coon, so check all plants in your home before bringing him home. While you may think putting a toxic plant up high and out of reach is sufficient, cats have a way of reaching even the most unreachable places. Simply rehoming your dangerous houseplant is a much safer option. Contact your vet right away if your kitten ingests a plant he shouldn't.

KEEP LIDS ON TRASH CANS – Unless you enjoy picking trash up from the floor, keep a lid on all trash cans in the home. Many cats will make a game out of knocking them over and scattering the remnants with their playful little paws.

PULL BACK BLIND CORDS – Pull cords that hang on window blinds are a tempting toy for a young kitten and even an adult cat. Be sure to pull those back or tie them up with a rubber band so that your Maine Coon cannot become dangerously tangled up.

Photo Courtesy of Meghan Rockey

Foods that are Dangerous to Cats

GRAPES – Grapes and raisins can cause serious illness for your Maine Coon, including kidney failure. Vomiting within twelve hours of ingestion, as well as lethargy, loss of appetite, decreased urination, abdominal pain, and diarrhea, can occur as warning signs. If your cat vomits after eating grapes or raisins, call the vet urgently for emergency care. While each individual cat will have a different tolerance level, even a small amount can make some cats seriously ill.

ONIONS AND GARLIC – Onions, garlic, and anything in the allium family, when consumed in substantial quantities, can cause anemia in cats. Symptoms include pale gums, lethargy, weakness, or orange to dark red urine. If you see any of these signs in your cat, you should seek immediate vet care.

DAIRY – Yes, this even includes milk! While not technically toxic to cats, most felines have a difficult time digesting lactose, meaning that bowl of warm milk you thought he would like may actually cause gastrointestinal upset and diarrhea.

RAW MEAT OR EGGS – Cats can be affected by E. coli poisoning or salmonella just as humans can. Keep the raw meat away from a curious cat when you're cooking.

CHOCOLATE – It's not just dogs that can't consume chocolate. In fact, it is equally toxic for cats. Chocolate contains methylxanthine, which is a stimulant that can stop a cat's metabolic process. Methylxanthines are found in especially high amounts in pure dark chocolate and baker's chocolate.

Too much methylxanthine causes seizures and irregular heart function, which can lead to death. If your cat ingests chocolate, call your emergency vet line for help. Unlike with dogs, it is not recommended to induce vomiting with hydrogen peroxide in cats, as this can cause ulcers.

XYLITOL – Xylitol is particularly dangerous to cats as it does not take much to cause a dangerous or deadly reaction. Vomiting is typically the initial symptom of xylitol poisoning. If you suspect there is a chance your cat has ingested even a small amount of xylitol, call the veterinarian immediately because time is critical, and liver failure is common.

This list of foods known to be toxic to cats is not comprehensive. You should always check with your trusted vet before deciding to feed your Maine Coon companion any human foods.

CHAPTER 5
Caring for Your Maine Coon Cat

Initial Health Care

When you first bring home your Maine Coon cat, he will need to see a vet fairly quickly for his initial health-care visit. This visit may be required and outlined in the breeder contract discussed in chapter 3. Be sure to bring any and all records you have from the breeder to this first appointment so that your vet can get the full scope of his care.

While you may be tempted to simply carry your loving feline in your arms as you take him to the vet, the safest and most effective way to travel with your cat is via a carrier. Place a small blanket with the smell of home inside and reassure your cat verbally as you transport him. Most cats will become nervous on trips outside of the home; however, a wellness check is important.

At this first vet visit, the veterinarian will give your cat a full check-up. This will include checking his weight, coat health, ears, eyes, and nose. He will also check for masses or abnormalities in the belly and examine joints. A stool sample may be taken to check for parasites as well. If your cat is due for inoculations, the vet will likely administer them at this time.

Indoor or Outdoor?

Unlike other domesticated pets, cats cannot be contained within a fence and kept in the safety of a backyard. In fact, according to Dr. John Bradshaw of the School of Veterinary Science at Bristol University, a domestic cat allowed to roam outdoors will often cover a territory of anywhere from 130 to 650 feet from the home, possibly farther.

BRINGING A NEW KITTEN HOME

JASMINA WALTZ
Star-Studded Maine Coons

"When the kitten arrives at home, put it in a safe place. This could be a large bathroom or a spare bedroom. The room should have all the necessary items that the kitten needs—food, water, litter, toys, and hopefully something that has a familiar scent on it. Spend as much time as possible with your kitten during this time."

"Place the carrier in the room and let the kitten come out when it feels comfortable doing so. Some kittens will come out right away. Others may take a bit longer. Never pull or force the kitten out of the carrier."

"The kitten should remain in the safe place for at least seven to 14 days (14 days if other pets are present). This is where the cat can get used to the sounds and smells of its new home without feeling overwhelmed."

"If there are other resident cats, you'll want to exchange scents before they meet. So, for example, leave something like a blanket, towel, etc. in the area of one cat for a few days and then bring that to the other cat's area. Do that for a few days. You can also rub a towel on one cat and then take that towel and rub it on the other cat. That will teach the animals that the smell is familiar and not a threat. Then swap the animals' spaces for a few hours. That will also help to familiarize them with the other cat's smell. Do all this for a few days before they see each other for the first time. Then use a carrier to place the new kitten in the room to see how your other cat reacts. Slow down with the introduction if there is a lot of animosity. Keep the animals both busy playing when you let the kitten out of the carrier. This will redirect your resident cat's attention to something other than the new kitten."

Many cat owners struggle to know if their cat should remain indoors at all times or be allowed outside. While many cat owners are encouraged to keep their cats exclusively indoors, especially in America, this is actually a fairly recent phenomenon.

Up until the 1950s, when cat litter was introduced, all cats had to go outside to relieve themselves, just as dogs do. There is great debate among cat enthusiasts as to which lifestyle is actually beneficial for a cat. We will outline some of the details below.

PHYSICAL WELL-BEING – Generally speaking, indoor cats typically face fewer physical risks day-to-day than their outdoor counterparts. This is due to the lack of predators and environmental risks within the walls of your home. Outdoor cats not only contend with predatory animals, traffic, and extreme

*Photo Courtesy
of Patrick Barneoud*

weather; they also may be subject to theft, falling from trees, and infectious diseases such as FIV, feline leukemia, and feline infectious peritonitis.

Outdoor cats will also be much more likely to hunt small animals on excursions. This often means killing wildlife and bringing it home as a trophy. While this is completely natural behavior, it may be off-putting to many owners.

While not entirely risk-free, cats that live within the home at all times have far fewer risk factors and depend on you to remove those risks, such as toxic houseplants, from the equation as much as possible.

FUN FACT
Water Lovers

While most cats seem to despise getting wet, many Maine Coons enjoy water. Due to their thick, somewhat water-resistant coats, Maine Coons tend not to be bothered by water and may enjoy playing in it. Some theories about the origin of this breed posit that Maine Coons are descended from domestic short-haired cats who bred with long-haired cats brought over from Europe by seafarers. So perhaps their affinity for water, or at least their water-resistant coat, comes from these early seafaring ancestors.

Aside from physical risks, you may also wish to consider the coat of your Maine Coon before deciding whether to keep him indoors or let him roam. With a long, silky coat, dirt and debris can make it much more difficult to keep your cat clean and well-groomed.

EMOTIONAL WELL-BEING – On the other side of the argument is the emotional well-being of the cat. While physical factors are important, so are emotional factors. Due to the monotonous and controlled environment in your home, your cat will likely not be able to exercise his natural hunting instincts or his innate desire to explore. This can often lead to boredom or even depression in your cat. Some signals that your cat may be frustrated can include increased and distressed vocalizations, poor behavior, increased scratching and destruction, and irritability.

If you feel your indoor cat is exhibiting signs of frustration or distress, try to introduce things to keep him active and mentally stimulated. Offer him several new toys, including some that stimulate the hunting instinct. This can be something as simple as a feather on a string.

In short summary, a cat is free to behave and act naturally as a cat when allowed to roam outdoors; however, this lifestyle poses greater physical risks and often shortens the expected lifespan of said cat. Talk to your breeder and your vet, and evaluate your own cat's unique situation before coming to a decision.

*Photo Courtesy
of Mike & Tami Brouillette*

Emotional Needs of the Maine Coon

> *They will want to spend their time bonding with you, not only out of fear, but to mark you as their own. They will be incredibly loving and affectionate, but please remember, if you have other animals, to keep them confined to a room for the first 30 days. Quarantine is very important, not just for medical reasons but for psychological reasons. We're unable to convey to our kittens why they are leaving, and we know it can be a terrifying experience, so we need families to do their best to make them feel safe, comfortable, and welcome.*
>
> KOSMOS L KNOVAS
> *KosmikCattery LLC*

The Maine Coon cat is one with high emotional and social needs. These dogs of the cat world love to be near and around their people consistently. Possessing what seems like an extra dose of curiosity, the Maine Coon is always curious as to what his owner is up to, frequently following him around to investigate.

If your Maine Coon is kneading and vocalizing his love for you, rest assured those are signals of his affection. While he may not always be a "lap cat," he enjoys your company and will certainly indulge in snuggles on his terms.

A Maine Coon left alone regularly for long periods of time can become lonely and depressed, which can lead to destructive behavior. If you cannot care for the high companionship and emotional needs of a Maine Coon cat, consider another breed instead.

A Safe Retreat

No matter if your cat is the lone pet in the house or if he shares a space with another cat or species, he will need access to a safe retreat. Cats are natural predators, but they are also prey. In the wild, a cat will often climb a tree to get a better view of his surroundings and give him a resting place where he can be out of sight and reach of predators. This same principle applies to the cat in your home.

Photo Courtesy of Diane Ingvarsson

No matter how few predators there are in your home, your Maine Coon should always have a place where he can go in times of stress or simply when he wants to be left alone. This may be at the top of a cat tower, or he may end up preferring the top shelf of your bedroom closet. Either way, when he retreats to one of these safe spots, leave him alone until he is ready to come out and socialize again. This is especially important if you have other animals such as dogs in your home.

How to Handle Scratching

Scratching can be the bane of a cat owner's existence, so much so that some owners opt to have their cats declawed. While your couch, carpet, and curtains all may bear the brunt of this patience-testing habit, in fact, scratching is a totally normal and instinctual behavior for cats.

There are several reasons why your cat may be scratching things around your home. These include marking something with his scent via the scent glands in his paws, filing down his nails, expressing excitement or stress, or even just stretching out his legs.

Regardless of why he is doing it, unfortunately, the behavior cannot and should not be stopped. Don't worry; that doesn't mean your sofa is doomed. We will outline several solutions to help you redirect the scratching to an approved area so both you and your Maine Coon can live harmoniously.

GET A SCRATCHING POST – Instead of trying to prevent scratching altogether, provide a safe and acceptable place for your cat to scratch that isn't destructive. A scratching post is a perfect solution. Some scratching posts are upright, and some are flat for floor scratching. Depending on your cat's preference, he may like to use one more than the other.

KEEP A SPRAY BOTTLE HANDY – If you're struggling to keep your cat from scratching something he shouldn't, keep a spray bottle full of water handy and give him a squirt in the face as you catch him in the act. Verbalize a firm "no" and then redirect him to his scratching pad or post.

PLACE SCRATCHING POSTS NEAR TROUBLE AREAS – Place the scratching post or pad near an area your cat loves to scratch. If he loves to scratch the sofa, place the post near the sofa as a convenient alternative. This can really help to break the bad habit quicker.

USE A COMMERCIAL SPRAY – There are many commercial sprays available at pet stores that are intended to help deter your cat from scratching a particular area. Just be sure to test the spray on an inconspicuous area before you use it on furniture or carpet.

A Case to Keep the Claws

Many cat owners become so fed up with scratching they resort to surgically removing their cat's claws through a process called declawing. This can be done on either the front claws or all four claws. While this may seem like an easy fix, it is actually detrimental to your cat for several reasons.

Photo Courtesy of Meghan Rockey

Claws are a cat's only defense mechanism, as well as a crucial part of their anatomy that helps with balance and mobility. Cats use their claws to protect themselves in a fight and also to climb up and away from predators. Without this defense, they are likely to become stressed and anxious, aware of their vulnerability. Even if your cat stays indoors, one accidental escape can be perilous when he's left outside defenseless.

Not only does removing his claws leave him defenseless from predators, but it can be incredibly painful and life-altering for a cat. When a cat's front claws are removed, he may adapt by shifting more weight to his back legs, causing him to feel out of balance. Declawing a cat is more than simply trimming the claws back; it is a surgical procedure that amputates the cat's toes up to the first joint, and it is irreversible.

Hairballs

Hairballs are another not-so-glorious aspect of cat ownership. While they can be gross-sounding and -looking, they are not dangerous. In fact, a hairball is simply a collection of hair that has formed into a "ball" in your cat's digestive system. This happens when your cat grooms himself. Much of the hair passes through his system and ends up in the litter box, but what doesn't ends up as a mass of hair that must come out another way.

Oftentimes you will know when your cat is trying to bring up a hairball because he will begin to gag and hack. These hairballs are not actually shaped like a ball but are instead tubular in shape and sometimes covered in a slimy substance. While it may sound distressing to an owner, typically, a cat will cough up a hairball then calmly walk away like nothing happened.

Healthy cats should not be coughing up a hairball every day or even every other day. Instead, this should happen approximately every month or so. If your cat is experiencing more hairballs than normal, you may want to see the vet to have him checked for digestive or skin issues.

Learning the Language

Maine Coons are said to have a language of their own. Meowing, chirping, chattering, and trilling—these vocalizations are a Maine Coon's way of communicating his needs and emotions. As you and your Maine Coon get to know each other, you will learn what each sound means and almost come to speak his language!

CHAPTER 6
Training and Socialization

> *Maine Coons are incredibly social creatures and are good around people, other pets, and enjoy being out with the family on events and trips. Always be mindful of your feline's social cues and have a safe space for it to go if necessary.*
>
> KOSMOS L KNOVAS
> *KosmikCattery LLC*

The Importance of Socialization

Though the Maine Coon cat is delightfully sociable and friendly by nature, early socialization is still important for both a Maine Coon kitten you bring home from a breeder and an adopted adult cat. If you're bringing home a kitten, early and frequent socialization is key to a well-rounded and affectionate cat, so introduce your kitten to the family as soon as you bring him home and shower him with affection. Carefully handle your Maine Coon kitten, but handle him often from a young age, so he is accustomed to it as he grows. These interactions early on will pave the way for a positive and trusting relationship between you and your Maine Coon for years to come.

While socializing a kitten is fairly easy, socializing an adult Maine Coon can be more challenging. If your cat has an unknown past or a history of trauma, socialization may not come naturally and may require patience and time. Be sure to follow the detailed steps outlined in chapter 4 to safely and properly introduce an adult cat to other animals in your home. Because your Maine Coon will likely not interact with any pets other than those in your home, it is not important to take your cat out to become adjusted to spending time with other animals.

> "
> *While it is still quite young, try to introduce your Maine Coon kitten to a variety of people and situations. The more people your Maine Coon sees as a kitten, the more socialized it will be as an adult. Maine Coons generally get along with dogs quite well, including very large dogs. However, putting them into homes with small dogs with high-pitched barking or dogs with a high prey drive should be avoided.*
>
> TERI MATZKIN
> *SaraJen Maine Coon Cats*
> "

If you are attempting to introduce an adult Maine Coon to the human members of your family, try to make the introduction calm and quiet as not to stress him out even more. Remember, your home is like a foreign world to your Maine Coon, and he will likely need time to adjust to the new sights and sounds. Hiding away and withdrawing for a period of time while he adjusts is normal and reasonable. Never force your cat out of his safe area.

As your cat becomes more comfortable in his new home, he may venture out of hiding to inspect the place. Try to let him do so without disturbing

Photo Courtesy of Linda Briggs

Photo Courtesy of Anita Greifenstein

him so he can gain confidence in his surroundings. If your cat approaches you or another member of the family, try not to reach out to him. Instead, allow him to sniff and inspect you as well, offering touch only if he offers first.

Although socializing an adult cat can be a challenge, Maine Coons are typically easier to socialize than other house cats and should adjust well to a happy and loving home.

> *I think if you really want a social cat, you should take your kitten out! Put your kitten in a carrier, especially one with wheels, or in a pet stroller. Walk all over your neighborhood and let the kitten hear the roar of traffic and get startled by everything new. Take the kitten to Home Depot or some other store and do the same. The more you expose a young kitten to lots of noise and people, the more well-adjusted it will be to things that are unusual.*
>
> SHERRY DELONY CAMPBELL
> *Mainesuspect Maine Coons*

Training a Cat?

> *Maine Coons are very unique and special because you can train them similarly to the way you would train a dog. Use verbal cues and treat them (food or petting) whenever they do something that you would like them to do. You can train your Maine Coon to sit, play fetch, and walk on a leash, among many other humorous activities!*
>
> LYNN BARNETT
> *Crescent Moon Maine Coons*

Cats often get a bad reputation for being aloof, stubborn, independent, and downright untrainable. Well, if you've ever owned a cat, you're probably chuckling right now because you know those descriptors are sometimes hard to argue with. Even so, Maine Coon cats, while still independent and stubborn at times, are actually highly intelligent and easily trainable.

Contrary to dogs, cats are not driven by praise and will not quickly respond to it during a training session. In fact, by nature, cats are not highly motivated to work in partnership with their humans like dogs are. This can present a unique challenge while training and is probably the number one reason people think their cats cannot be trained.

Positive Reinforcement and Clicker Training Basics

Cats do not respond to punishment or negative reinforcement. Instead, reward them with a treat they love to encourage them to do a certain task. When positively reinforcing an action, there are two types of reinforcements used, primary and secondary.

PRIMARY REINFORCEMENT: Primary reinforcements are directly related to the basic needs of your cat. These are things like food and water. This does not mean food and water are withheld until obedience is achieved; rather, the technique employs extra rewards like food and training treats as primary reinforcements. Treats made specifically for training are small and high-reward.

Photo Courtesy
of Annemarie van Beek

SECONDARY REINFORCEMENT:
Secondary reinforcements are things not based on basic needs but rather on learned social constructs. These things include verbal praise, smiles, rubs, and anything else your cat has learned means you're pleased. Secondary reinforcements typically do not motivate a cat the way primary reinforcements do and are often ineffective.

There is a second type of secondary reinforcement called conditioned reinforcement. This includes otherwise neutral sounds and objects like a clicker. When used in conjunction with primary reinforcements, these objects become positive by association. Conditioned reinforcement can be effective initially but can lose effectiveness when the primary reinforcement is taken away.

> 66
>
> *As with most cats, when attempting to train a Maine Coon, punishment is not the ticket. When it is doing something you'd rather it didn't, try to give the cat an alternative activity to displace its attention. For example, provide attractive, comfortable places to scratch, such as a sturdy cat tree, so the Maine Coon does not have to resort to taking care of its nails on your furniture. The cat will learn this quite easily in most cases and be happy not to be scolded while lounging on its tree. Maine Coons are intelligent and can often be trained to do certain activities/skills by employing food treats—just be sure they are healthy treats!*
>
> TERI MATZKIN
> *SaraJen Maine Coon Cats*
>
> 99

With enough determination and ample patience on your part, your cat can learn to do several tricks, including coming when called, sitting, and even giving high-fives. We'll walk you through each command step by step so you and your Maine Coon can get started today.

COME – This command is simple and should be relatively easy to accomplish. Simply show your cat his favorite high-reward treat from a distance, call his name, and say, "come." When he comes to you, reward him with a treat, verbal praise, and a click if you are using the clicker. Repeat and practice this for about 10 minutes before giving your cat a break. Eventually, your cat will learn to associate the command and the action and will obey without the need for a treat each time.

SIT – For this command, get in front of your cat and have him facing you. Hold a treat in front of his nose and slowly raise it up and over his head toward his tail, so he is forced to sit down and look up. Give the verbal command "sit" as you do this. When he sits, reward him with a treat and a phrase such as "yes" or "good." If you're training with a clicker, also give a click when he obeys the command.

HIGH-FIVE – For this command, hold a treat in your palm but cover it with your fingers in a fist. Hold your hand up in front of your cat. As your cat paws at your hand to try to retrieve the treat, give the verbal "high-five" and then reward him with the treat.

No matter what command you are working on, keep training sessions focused on one trick at a time and train for no longer than 10 to 15 minutes. This will keep your cat interested and make training much easier for you. Not only does training stimulate your cat mentally, it can help grow the bond and loving relationship between you and your Maine Coon.

HELPFUL TIP
Choosing a Cat Perch

Cat trees and perches are a vital part of your cat's social life, providing a safe, protected space to regroup and relax. When choosing a perch for your Maine Coon, be sure that you choose something that is not only large enough for your kitty, but also sturdy enough to support its weight. Generally, cats don't enjoy it when their legs dangle off the side of a perch, so be sure that if the perch doesn't have sides, the platform is big enough for your Maine Coon to fit. Window seats, cat trees, and cat condos are all excellent options for keeping your cat happy and relaxed.

CHAPTER 7

All About the Litter Box

The litter box is the thing that no cat owner loves to talk about, but every cat owner deals with. If you're new to cat ownership, we'll show you everything you need to know about litter boxes, so you are well prepared before you bring your Maine Coon cat home. After all, we all have to go somewhere!

Types of Boxes

> Find out what the breeder used both for style of litter box and type of litter and don't veer much from that initially. If you are wedded to change, get a second box, and once it's regularly used, you can eliminate the first.
>
> SHERRY DELONY CAMPBELL
> *Mainesuspect Maine Coons*

When it comes to choosing a litter box for your Maine Coon cat, size matters. Due to the size of the breed, they require some of the largest litter boxes around. Aside from size, though, how will you know what litter box is best when there are so many different kinds available?

LITTER PANS – These basic litter boxes are exactly what they sound like—simple open pans full of litter. These boxes are about as basic as they come and can even be found at local dollar stores in a pinch. While nothing fancy, they get the job done.

Some litter pans have attachable rims to raise the side wall height to prevent litter from flying. These may or may not make a difference, depending on how messy your cat is with the litter.

HOODED LITTER BOX – A basic hooded litter box is just a litter pan with a hood and a door or opening for your cat to enter. These boxes provide a bit more privacy for your cat when he is doing his business. The side walls also keep most litter from being shoveled out by those digging kitty paws.

One con to a covered litter box is the extra trouble it takes to clean it out. You either have to reach through the opening with a scoop or remove the top entirely.

TOP-ENTRY BOXES – These boxes take up about the same amount of space as the hooded pans; however, the entry point is on the top instead of the side. This can greatly reduce the amount of litter that is tracked outside of the box and contains almost all of the litter kicked around inside.

Top-entry boxes are also great for deterring some dogs from digging in them because the entry point is difficult for them to reach through.

SELF-CLEANING LITTER BOX – These magical boxes were designed to take the grunt work out of doing kitty doo-ty. They contain rakes on motors, and they will periodically sweep the box and deposit anything caught into a bin. All you have to do is empty the bin periodically, and your litter box remains clean. These boxes start with a price tag of about $150, and they go up from there depending on the brand and features.

ROBOTIC LITTER BOXES – Similar to self-cleaning boxes, the robot litter box takes it one step further. These litter boxes look like futuristic space capsules and can sense when your cat leaves the box. After a certain amount of time, the box actually rotates and separates the clump from the clean litter, dropping the waste into a fully sealed waste bin.

HELPFUL TIP
Bigger is Usually Better

Maine Coon cats are one of the largest domestic cat breeds, so it's no surprise that they require a larger than average litter box to fit their needs. A Maine Coon's litter box should be at least 18 by 20 inches, but this size can vary based on your cat's preference. Like any cat, litter box preference can be a process of trial and error. But how will you know if your cat doesn't like the box or boxes you've provided? Out-of-the-box accidents are usually the first and best clue that something isn't right. When it comes to litter boxes, bigger is generally better.

While this box is a cat owner's dream, it will cost you significantly. With a price tag of almost $600, this box is a luxury.

BOXES THAT LOOK LIKE FURNITURE – If you're not sure where to put your cat's litter box, and you can't find an inconspicuous spot, a litter box that looks like a piece of furniture may be the perfect way to hide one in plain sight. These boxes are often made to look like side tables and have a place to put a pan or hooded litter box inside. These can be a great option for someone who doesn't want the eyesore of a traditional litter box sitting in their home.

Litter Options

Once you have your chosen litter box, it's time to fill it. But much like the boxes themselves, one walk down the litter aisle at the pet store can leave you confused and uncertain. Beware that even if you choose one litter, your Maine Coon very well may decide he doesn't like it, and you may be forced to try another. This trial and error is natural and just part of the learning curve when bringing a new cat home.

CLUMPING VS. NON-CLUMPING – Basic cat litter comes in two styles: clumping and non-clumping. Basically, clumping cat litter will form clumps around your cat's urine, making it scoopable and easier to remove from the box without replacing the whole bin of litter. For ease of cleaning, scoopable, clumpable litter is the best way to go.

SCENTED OR NON-SCENTED – In order to try to mask the smell, some litter comes in a scented variety. Your cat may or may not tolerate the smell of scented cat litter.

While clay is the most commonly used ingredient in cat litter, it is not the only option. Many companies have engineered litter specifically to address issues such as eco-friendliness, excessive dust, tracking, and other common litter complaints.

If you are searching for a more eco-friendly and biodegradable litter option, try corn, wood pellets, coconut husks, wheat, walnut shells, recycled newspaper, and even silica-based crystals. While these are great for the environment, they are typically more expensive and do not clump like traditional clumping clay litter. This can make cleaning out the litter box a bit more challenging.

PRETTY LITTER – Pretty Litter is a brand of silica cat litter that claims to be able to tell you things about your cat's health by changing colors based on urine. If the litter turns blue, it may indicate a urinary tract infection. If it turns orange, it can indicate metabolic acidosis or kidney tubular acidosis. If it's red, that can point toward a lower urinary tract disorder or other kidney diseases.

Many happy Pretty Litter customers claim the litter was their first indication something was wrong with their cat. If you are the type of Maine Coon owner that loves peace of mind, Pretty Litter may be just what you need.

Once you've chosen a type of litter, place your box where it will stay and fill it with two to three inches of litter. Your Maine Coon will love to dig and claw at the litter, so don't skimp. As your cat uses the box, it will need to be scooped daily to keep it clean and fresh.

Litter Box Training

> "
> If you're getting your Maine Coon from a breeder, hopefully it will already be litter trained; however, sometimes that's not the case. If your cat is not litter trained, try keeping it in a smaller room with a litter box, food/water, toys, etc. Set your cat in the litter box and dig its feet in the litter. When it goes outside the litter box, pick it up and put some of it in the litter box. There are also products that you can put in a litter box that will help attract the cat to that space. Time, consistency, and patience are crucial. Most cats will pick it up fairly quickly. It's also best if you start out using the same litter as the breeder or rescue until the cat learns where the litter box is.
>
> JENNIFER JINKINS
> *Kaiju Maine Coon Cattery*
> "

Luckily, most kittens learn how to use the litter box from their mom before they leave the litter. Even if they don't, cats possess a strong instinctual urge to cover their waste, and the litter box is the perfect place to do just that. If your cat is not automatically using the litter box, there are a couple of things you can do to help him learn.

INTRODUCE HIM TO THE BOX – As soon as you bring your cat home, formally show him the litter box. Make sure you don't move the box, so he always knows where it is. If you do, reintroduce your cat to the box in the new location as soon as you move it.

ENCOURAGE YOUR CAT TO GO – After meals or after he drinks a lot of water, place your cat or kitten into the litter box. He may or may not need to go, but if he does, reward him with a treat and verbal praise.

Make sure not to scold your cat for any accidents that happen while he is learning. This will only make relieving himself more stressful and further confusion. Simply continue the steps above and have patience.

Common Problems

> *Do not punish your kitten or rub its nose in the mess if it goes potty outside of the litter box. Try to intervene if you see the kitten doing this and place it in the litter box. Always praise your kitten and give it positive attention when it successfully uses the litter box. You may also give the kitten a treat. Ask your breeder or rescue what cat litter it is currently using. Do not switch the brand or type of litter until the kitten is comfortable in your home. Some cats do not like covered litter boxes and will not use them. Clumping litter can be dangerous for kittens under four months old. Kittens are curious and may taste the litter or lick it off their fur when they are grooming themselves. If they ingest too much, it can cause an intestinal blockage that will require emergency surgery.*

> CORIE AND MATTHEW HELMS
> *Rocketmans Maine Coons*

Oftentimes, if you find that your cat is not using the litter box properly, there is a reason. Cats are particularly picky about where they do their business, so if something is off, they may refuse to use it at all.

DIRTY LITTER BOX – One common reason cats go outside of the litter box is that it's too dirty for their liking. Going too long between cleanings may make your sweet Maine Coon boycott the box until it's cleaned.

NOT ENOUGH LITTER – Sometimes, if the box gets low on litter and you can see the bottom of the pan, a cat will refuse to use it. Keep an eye on the box and make sure it stays full and clean to avoid issues.

SWITCH IT UP – If your cat is suddenly not using his litter box, he may simply not like the litter you chose. Try switching to a different kind or use unscented rather than scented. Eventually, you will find one he is willing to use.

NO PRIVACY – Every cat is different, and while some love to be able to see their surroundings while doing their business, others love their privacy and would prefer a conspicuous space. If your cat is having trouble using the box in a highly trafficked area, try moving it to a more private location to see if that helps.

TOO SMALL – As discussed above, Maine Coon cats are large and will need ample space in a litter box. If your cat looks cramped inside the box, he would probably appreciate you sizing up.

Toxoplasmosis

Toxoplasmosis is a parasite that can infect both cats and animals. Cats can get these parasites from being outside and catching and killing wild animals such as birds. While many cats are infected with toxoplasmosis, it usually does not cause serious illness in cats or humans.

Cats shed toxoplasmosis through their feces, meaning it is possible to contract the parasite by improper handling of the litter box. If a human does get sick from toxoplasmosis, the person is likely to not even know, but it is possible someone may experience flu-like symptoms for up to two weeks.

The real risk from toxoplasmosis is for pregnant mothers. Pregnant mothers exposed to cat litter infected with toxoplasmosis are at a higher risk of miscarriage, as well as birth defects, brain damage, and blindness. For this reason, pregnant women should never handle cat litter. If you are pregnant and you must handle the litter box, wear gloves and wash your hands thoroughly afterward.

CHAPTER 8
Grooming Your Maine Coon Cat

Brushing

> 66
>
> *Get your Maine Coon used to being brushed and combed. I rec-ommend brushing and combing at night while sitting on the sofa watching TV. Be very gentle, more like you are caressing the cat than grooming. Let the cat think this is love, not a chore. Also, this is when you should clip nails. I recommend you clip the cat's nails once a week. If you are dedicated to grooming and clipping nails, your cat will become used to it and will expect it.*
>
> **SHERRY DELONY CAMPBELL**
> *Mainesuspect Maine Coons*
>
> 99

The long, beautiful coat is the calling card of the Maine Coon breed. This beautiful coat definitely comes with responsibility, however. In order to keep your cat's coat clean and mat-free, he will need regular brushing at least twice a week, possibly more if he's prone to matting.

Using a grooming rake will help remove any loose hair from your cat's coat that may otherwise get caught and cause matting. Be sure to get his underside as well, as this is where matting is most common. Not only will regular brushing keep your Maine Coon's coat clean and in tip-top shape, but it will also cut back on the amount of shedding you have to contend with in your home.

Bathing

How often you bathe your Maine Coon cat will depend on whether he is an exclusively indoor cat or if he spends some of his time outside. If your cat lives indoors only, he really shouldn't need baths very often. Cats do a remarkable and efficient job of cleaning themselves.

If your cat ventures outside for any amount of time, is obese and cannot reach some areas, or is elderly, you may find that he needs assistance bathing a bit more frequently. Between outdoor smells, debris, and other messes your cat may get into, bathing can help keep his beautiful long coat clean and healthy.

When bathing your Maine Coon, you will need a brush, tub, shampoo, and a hand sprayer or a large cup. Be sure you only use a cat-specific shampoo and never use human shampoo, as it is much too harsh for your cat's delicate skin. Look for a shampoo that is free of fragrance, parabens, and sulfates.

Begin by brushing your cat's coat with a slicker brush. This can help to remove any large debris and loose fur beforehand. Next, fill a tub with a few inches of lukewarm water and gently set your cat into it. If your cat is not a fan of water or baths, you may want to wear a pair of rubber gloves to protect your hands and arms from scratches.

Once your cat is in the water, wet his coat with a hand sprayer or a large cup, avoiding his eyes and ears. Due to his thick fur, it may take a minute to fully soak his coat. Lather the shampoo in your hands and gently massage into your cat, avoiding his face and ears, and then rinse completely. Be sure to follow the directions on the bottle of your chosen shampoo.

There are also several rinse-free shampoo options for cats that may be a good solution for a Maine Coon that needs a refresher but not a full bath. These can be applied right after brushing to give your cat a nice clean, fresh scent without the stress of a bath.

> **"**
>
> *Maine Coons dump a seasonal coat every four months. Regular brushing keeps the hair in control, is a fun activity, and lessens the amount of hair cats have to swallow. If you cannot bathe your cat every four to six months, then find a vet that has grooming facilities. Starting cats young helps them accept bathing. Using a vet facility is safest for your pet in the event of an emergency.*
>
> MICKEY COLE
> *Maine Delite Cattery*
>
> **"**

Drying Your Maine Coon

With a coat as long and thick as the Maine Coon's, it is important to dry your cat's coat after a bath. Begin by using your hands to rub any excess water out of his coat. Do this until you can't get any more water out. Next, wrap your Maine Coon in a warm towel and gently pat him dry. You may need several warm towels on hand so you can replace the wet towels with dry ones. Warming the towels in a towel warmer or dryer before can help your cat stay warm while his fur is drying.

If your cat will tolerate it, you may want to blow dry his coat. Be aware that many cats will not appreciate the blow dryer. If you do decide to use a blow dryer, keep it on the cool air setting so you don't burn your cat. If your cat is not a fan, stick to towel drying so as not to stress him out further.

Many cats, no matter how much they may love water, will not enjoy being bathed. Begin early and slowly to get your Maine Coon accustomed to the process and reward him often with treats. This can help get him comfortable and create a positive association with bathing.

*Photo Courtesy
of Michelle and Donald Sharp*

Trimming or Clipping

> "
>
> *Brush from day one to get cats used to being groomed. They will enjoy the attention and won't try to get away from you when they are older. Trim the breeches area since some cats like to sit in their litter box when urinating. Their bibs get wet. Brush cats a few times a week to prevent mats.*
>
> KELLY SPARKMAN
> *Mountain Fork European Maine Coons*
>
> "

Sometimes Maine Coon owners choose to have their cat's fur trimmed or clipped in some areas. The main reason to have your cat's fur trimmed would be for hygiene purposes. If he tends to get feces stuck to his backside fur, you may want to keep that area trimmed shorter. Also, if your cat tends to get mats in certain areas, such as under the belly or the armpits, you may choose to trim his fur a bit in those areas as well.

In extreme cases, some opt to give their cat a lion's cut. This cut is very dramatic in appearance, essentially shaving the entirety of the cat except for his head, neck, a portion of his legs, and a puff on the end of his tail.

This cut is very controversial as some believe it can cause psychological and even physical damage to your cat. Shaving your Maine Coon exposes him to the elements. A cat's fur doesn't only keep him warm in the winter; it also helps regulate his temperature in the summer, as well as protects his skin from the sun, bugs, and even predators. Without his beautiful coat, your Maine Coon will feel vulnerable. A lion's cut takes about four to six months to grow out, making this type of cut a long-term decision for you and your feline friend.

Trimming your cat's fur should only be done out of necessity and not for style, as it can be a traumatic experience for your cat. If you find a mat in your cat's fur while brushing, a quick snip can easily remedy the issue. However, if your Maine Coon is matted in several areas, it is advised you seek a professional for help. While some Maine Coons tolerate being groomed very well, others will not. Do not try to trim your cat's fur yourself if you are not an experienced groomer. Not only could you give your beautiful Maine Coon a bad haircut, but you might accidentally injure yourself or him.

*Photo Courtesy
of Liz Holmes
Monster Maine Coons*

Ear and Eye Care

Maine Coons do not need their ears cleaned often, but a periodic cleaning can keep them free of discharge and debris. To clean your cat's ears, simply pour a few drops of ear cleaning solution into each ear and gently massage at the base. With a clean cotton ball, wipe the ears clean.

Your Maine Coon's eyes should generally be clear; however, a little mucus or discharge can easily be removed with an eye cleaning wipe. These wipes can be found at any local pet store and work well for a quick and easy clean. If your cat is suffering from persistent eye discharge, seek vet care, as this can be a sign of infection.

Finding a Groomer

The stunning coat of a Maine Coon shouldn't be left in the hands of just any groomer. Do ample research and find a reputable groomer with Maine Coon experience. If you're not sure where to take your cat, ask for a vet referral. It is also wise to check online sites such as Google or Yelp to read reviews before choosing.

Be aware that some groomers use sedatives on cats. When used properly, these sedative drugs can be safe; however, there are always risks involved, and it's important to know a groomer's policy beforehand.

Claw Care

Your Maine Coon can do a pretty efficient job of taking care of his own claws. In fact, that's exactly what he's doing when he starts scratching away at your carpet or couch. This scratching helps to shed the dead layers of the old claw so the new, sharper claws can be exposed.

While it is not always necessary to trim your cat's claws, some believe it can be beneficial, depending on your Maine Coon's individual situation. If your cat lives exclusively indoors, he may have a harder time keeping his claws filed back naturally. This is usually achieved by scratching on rough surfaces outdoors, such as trees. While your indoor feline companion cannot access the same natural nail files, a good-quality scratching pad or post inside can serve the same purpose and keep him from filing his nails on the furniture.

Scratching Post 101

Because scratching is a vital and natural part of cat ownership, it's important to provide your Maine Coon with a safe place to do it, preferably one that isn't your furniture or home. There are several products on the market for scratching, yet there is no single right choice. Every cat will have his own preference for both orientation and material.

Photo Courtesy of Diane Ingvarsson

Post vs Pad

A scratching post is upright and allows your cat to reach up and scratch. A pad is much lower and lies on the ground or sits at a low angle. These pads allow your cat to reach forward and pull back with his claws. You may not know which your Maine Coon will prefer, but he will probably give you clues to help you determine.

If your Maine Coon has a tendency to scratch on the carpet or rugs, he may prefer a scratching pad more than an upright post. If he is reaching up to claw the furniture or the walls, he will probably want to use a scratching post. Try one of each if you aren't sure, and let him decide.

Scratching Material

Once you decide on a pad versus post, you'll need to choose a material. Scratchers come in several materials, including cardboard, rope, and carpet. Again, it may take some trial and error to know which texture your feline friend will like the best.

No matter which material you choose, your post or pad should be long enough or tall enough to accommodate your cat fully stretched out. For a cat the size of a Maine Coon, this means you will need a large scratching surface.

Trimming the Claws

If your indoor cat is scratching at things in your home, even with ample scratching areas provided, you may want to consider trimming his claws to protect your things. Having his nails trimmed doesn't come naturally to your cat, so take the time when he's very young to gently handle his paws so that he becomes accustomed to it. You may also want to keep a pair of cat-specific nail trimmers in sight so that he isn't frightened by the tool.

There are two main types of nail trimmers available for cats. These are the scissor-style trimmers and the guillotine trimmers. Either type works, and what you choose to use is simply based on preference and comfort of use.

Choose a time when your Maine Coon is relaxed and sleepy to attempt a nail trim. Place him in your lap and stroke his fur, keeping him calm and at ease. Gently hold his paw and squeeze with your thumb on top and your pointer finger on his paw pad. This gentle squeezing motion on each pad should extend the claws so you can trim them.

If your cat is leery of you handling his paws, reward him with treats and praise for allowing you to touch them. Do not try to trim his nails if he seems scared or distressed in any way. Instead, practice extending his claws with your fingers, praising him and rewarding him with treats to establish a positive association.

Once your Maine Coon is fully comfortable, follow the directions for your nail trimmers and clip your cat's nails. Look closely at your cat's claws before cutting and note where the quick is. This is the pink part of his claw where the blood supply is. Do not ever cut near the quick, as this is very painful and will cause bleeding. Instead, trim only the thin, narrow part of your cat's claw that curls down. It is better to trim less than to accidentally cut into the quick. If you do cut the quick, make sure you have some styptic powder on hand to stop the bleeding.

Only trim as many nails as your cat will allow. It's okay if you only trim a few at each sitting. Wait until your cat is calm and come back to get the rest when he is comfortable with it.

HELPFUL TIP
Choosing the Right Brush

Maine Coons are a long-haired breed and can be prone to developing matting. The best way to combat matting in your cat's fur is to establish a regular grooming routine with the appropriate brushes. An effective grooming routine will also decrease hairballs and shedding and create a strong bond between you and your ca t. Good brushes for Maine Coons include de-shedding brushes, slicker brushes, and de-matting combs. Brushing should be done two to three times per week for best results.

CHAPTER 9

Feeding Your Maine Coon

> "
>
> *Ideally, Maine Coons should be large and heavy cats, but the weight should come from well-toned muscle and not fat. To keep your Maine Coon toned, provide frequent opportunities for play and chasing, preferably on a lateral plane and not jumping high into the air. Feed a high meat protein diet (not fish), and feed more wet food than dry. Maine Coons can benefit greatly by having some amount of raw meat in their diet, which contributes greatly to muscle tone and overall health. Provide lots of fresh water, preferably from a type of flowing, filtered pet fountain. Use treats sparingly, and be sure they are healthy treats, such as freeze-dried meats, with no additives. Throwing these treats for Maine Coons to chase and, often, retrieve, is a great way to incorporate exercise into the day.*
>
> TERI MATZKIN
> *SaraJen Maine Coon Cats*
>
> "

Benefits of Quality Nutrition

Feeding your Maine Coon a quality diet is crucial for keeping his health in good shape. Proper nutrition is the best way to set your cat up for a healthy life from kittenhood on. Just as humans do their best to avoid processed foods and additives, the same principle applies to your cat.

Cats require a very specific balance of protein, fats, carbs, vitamins, and minerals to thrive. Choose a quality cat food that will provide him with everything he needs without any added fillers or preservatives. While there are many cat food options on the market, many are made as cheaply as possible and just meet minimum quality standards. While technically, your cat will be sustained on this type of food, it does not promote a healthy lifestyle.

*Photo Courtesy
of Douglas Grenville*

In the Wild

> *Feed wet food for longevity. Cats' ancestors were desert dwellers. They don't consume enough water on their own. Also, dry kibble tends to absorb moisture in the GI tract, which leads to dehydration and ends up with a cat dying prematurely from renal failure. Add water to pâté canned food. Add feline specialty soup/broth pouches to pâté food or kibble. It adds moisture and promotes hydration. Add a water fountain or allow running water to drip in the bathroom sink. Cats play in it and consume it more eagerly.*
>
> **KELLY SPARKMAN**
> *Mountain Fork European Maine Coons*

Cats are true carnivores and get most of their nutrition from small mammals and birds in the wild. While you probably don't want your Maine Coon bringing home dinner from the backyard, it's important that the food you choose to feed him provides him with the same nutrients. Cats eat almost no carbs in the wild, and any commercial food you buy should reflect that.

Types of Commercial Food

Commercial cat food comes in two main varieties, dry and wet. As a new cat owner, it can be overwhelming trying to choose. In this section, we'll discuss the basics of each type of food so you can make an informed decision on what's best for your Maine Coon.

DRY CAT FOOD – Dry cat food is typically created by combining ingredients and cooking at a very high temperature under pressure. It is shelf-stable after opening, has a minimal smell, and is typically cheaper than its wet counterpart.

Though convenience is a factor, dry cat food has been linked to obesity, possibly because many cats are "free fed" or allowed to graze from a full bowl all day. This can easily lead to overeating without the owner noticing. If you choose to feed your cat dry food, be sure to measure out how much he needs per day so you can track his nutrition.

It is also thought that much of the nutrition in dry cat food is depleted due to the extreme temperature it is cooked at. One pro to dry cat food,

73

however, is the cleanliness of it and the lack of smell. Wet foods can sometimes stick to your cat's long fur, meaning he may require a wipe down after each meal.

WET CAT FOOD – Wet cat food contains about 70 percent water as opposed to the 10 percent moisture content in dry food. This is a major benefit for cats who may not drink enough water on their own. Since cats, in general, are prone to kidney disease, the extra water content in wet cat food can really make a difference.

Canned wet cat food is also a great choice for a picky eater. It usually has a much stronger odor than dry food and can often bring your Maine Coon running with just one whiff. While this is a pro for your cat, it may be a con for you. Wet cat food can smell off-putting to owners and spoils much quicker, meaning if your cat doesn't finish his food pretty quickly, it will need to be refrigerated or tossed out.

Another con of wet cat food is the price. It is typically more costly per serving than dry food. However, for cats that have teeth problems or elderly cats, wet food may be easier for them to chew.

HELPFUL TIP
Houseplant Management

With the Maine Coon's large size, you may need to get creative with cat-proofing your houseplants. A simple stand might not be enough to deter a determined cat. Since some indoor houseplants are toxic to cats, it's best to take an inventory of your plants before bringing a cat into your life. If you don't want to dispose of the toxic varieties, you can try several mitigation methods. Cat deterrent spray is one option. Spray your plants with one of these commercially available sprays to make poisonous plants less appealing. Providing edible plant varieties in an accessible area for your cat can also discourage chewing on toxic plants.

COMBINATION OF FOOD – Many experts suggest that cats actually enjoy change and think it could be beneficial to mix it up, offering both a wet and dry variety. Mix the two types of food into one bowl or serve them at separate times. Either way, be sure to discard or refrigerate the uneaten wet food within a few hours of opening.

No matter what type of food you choose, check that it meets Association of American Feed Control Officials (AAFCO) standards. They set a baseline nutritional standard for all cat foods. Any food you choose for your Maine Coon should meet these standards at a bare minimum.

> There are always going to be many opinions on what the best food is for Maine Coons, but high protein and plenty of water are a must. Whether you decide to make your own raw blend or buy canned or dry kibble, grain-free or not, always know your ingredients. Chicken is not the same as chicken by-product. My cats are fed a can of food every morning and evening, and I let them free feed dry kibble as they choose until they are two years old. Once they are two years old, they grow at a much slower rate so I don't let them free feed during the day; if they are hungry, I give them a frozen raw nugget as a snack. Primal Raw frozen nuggets are high in protein, without a lot of fillers, and it is usually enough to keep them satisfied until dinner.
>
> JENNIFER JINKINS
> *Kaiju Maine Coon Cattery*

Ingredients to Avoid

> "
>
> *Dry food isn't really good for cats. Cats are obligate carnivores, which is just a fancy way of saying they must eat meat and hardly need any carbohydrates. Meat, meat, meat. Not corn or wheat or soy or potato or pea—not carrots or blueberries. All of those ingredients are just filler as the cat can't use the nutrition.*
>
> SHERRY DELONY CAMPBELL
> *Mainesuspect Maine Coons*
>
> "

Aside from knowing what ingredients your cat needs to thrive, it's important you also know which ingredients to avoid. Two of these red-flag ingredients include chemical preservatives such as BHT and BHA. These two chemicals help to preserve dry cat food, but they are suspected to be cancer-causing. It is best to avoid these ingredients at all costs for the long-term safety of your Maine Coon.

Another ingredient to be on the lookout for is any kind of meat by-product. These may also be labeled as meat meal and concentrate meal. These by-products are unidentified and inferior to true primary proteins. This low-quality ingredient is an indicator of an inferior food.

Carbohydrate fillers such as wheat and cornmeal are other ingredients to avoid. As discussed above, cats in the wild do not eat carbohydrates, so your cat food should not be full of them either. These are a cheap filler and signify a low-quality food. While most cat foods do contain some grain, the grain content should be much less than the protein content.

If your cat develops a gluten allergy or a sensitivity to grains, a quality grain-free cat food can be fed instead. Symptoms of grain allergies include itchiness, fur loss, and intestinal problems. Though not common, if these symptoms arise, seek vet care for your cat.

Table Food for Your Maine Coon

While it's not wise to feed an overweight or sick cat table food, there are some foods that are safe to share with your loving Maine Coon. Below is a list of approved table treats he may want to indulge in occasionally.

MEAT, FISH, AND EGGS: Since cats are true carnivores, they will most likely love sharing a bite of your cooked chicken or other animal products. You may even find your cat sniffing around your plate of salmon if you're not careful! Remember, share any table food in moderation and never share anything that is heavily spiced, as this may cause intestinal upset.

VEGETABLES AND FRUIT: Many cats won't be interested in vegetables or fruits, but if your cat shows interest, it's okay to share a bite or two. Cats cannot taste sweetness, so there likely won't be much appeal for fruits, but the vitamin, mineral, and water content are all beneficial for your feline companion as long as they don't take the place of a balanced cat food.

Table Foods to Avoid

While some table foods are okay to share with your fluffy friend, there are some you need to avoid due to potential toxicity. These include onions and garlic, chocolate, grapes and raisins, and raw dough. These foods can be harmful to your cat and should never be fed to him.

Other foods to avoid are dairy and milk. These are not dangerous for your cat; however, many cats cannot digest lactose and can suffer from intestinal upset. Dog food is another thing you shouldn't feed your Maine Coon. Eating it once isn't going to hurt him, but dog food isn't formulated to meet a cat's nutritional needs and cannot be fed in place of a quality cat food.

Weight Management

> *A high protein diet is important, as is making sure your cat doesn't get overweight. Weigh your cat regularly, get regular vet checks, and don't forget to keep your cat active with toys and playtime. Use a body condition chart to see if your cat is in a healthy range. Kittens can eat as much as they want, but it's important to keep an eye on the adults. Too much weight can cause many health problems for cats.*
>
> JASMINA WALTZ
> *Star-Studded Maine Coons*

An overweight cat is susceptible to many health issues and problems, such as arthritis, diabetes, and heart disease, that may be lessened by an appropriate body mass index. If you're unsure if your Maine Coon is overweight, your vet will be able to tell you. If he is, there are several lifestyle changes you can implement to help control your cat's weight.

The first thing you can do to promote weight loss for your cat is to stop all treats and table foods. Limit his feedings to mealtime only and cut out any additional calories. Another easy step you can take to manage his weight is to stop free grazing. Measure out his food to the appropriate amount and allow him to eat at mealtime only rather than letting him munch from a full bowl whenever he gets the urge.

Aside from food regulation, exercise is a great way to help your cat lose weight. Make it fun by engaging your Maine Coon with toys and encouraging him to get up and move around the house with you. You can even use a flashlight or a laser to exercise your cat if you're less mobile yourself.

If increased exercise and food regulation isn't working, your vet may recommend a weight-management cat food. These foods are formulated to help your cat shed extra weight while still getting all the vital nutrients he needs to thrive.

CHAPTER 10

Your Maine Coon's Healthcare Needs

Regular Vet Visits

Your Maine Coon will need to see the vet at regular intervals, about every twelve months, to make sure he is in good health. These visits are preventative and are intended to catch any issues before they become severe. These check-ups can also help you monitor your cat's weight and keep him up to date on vaccinations. Once your cat reaches senior status, around the age of seven to eleven, your vet may recommend twice-a-year visits to check on things in the case of any age-related diseases.

At these regular vet visits or wellness checks, your vet will give your Maine Coon a full look-over. This includes a general assessment of the cat's appearance, including alertness, his coat condition, and an evaluation of his gait and his weight. The vet will also check your Maine Coon's eyes, ears, nose, and throat, listen to his heart and lungs, and feel his abdomen and throat for painful lumps or swelling. If your cat is in need of any vaccinations or boosters, he will probably receive them during these wellness visits.

Make sure you come to these visits prepared with any questions or concerns you may have about your Maine Coon, no matter how small.

Choosing a Vet

It is wise to have a vet chosen for your Maine Coon before you even bring him home, as many breeders will stipulate that he sees a vet within the first few days of picking him up.

The best way to find a reputable vet in your area is to ask around among other cat owners you know. Word of mouth is a great and reliable way to get a feel for how clinics treat their patients. If you don't know anyone with a cat or aren't sure who to ask, check reviews for each clinic online via Google or Yelp.

Once you have found a few clinics you feel comfortable with, don't be afraid to call each office with questions before settling on one. Consider how much experience they have with Maine Coons, how far they are from your home, and general pricing. Ask them how they can be reached after hours in an emergency—an excellent vet doesn't do you much good if he cannot be reached after hours.

Do your best to find a reputable and reliable vet close to home. The last thing you will want to do if an emergency arises is drive your Maine Coon for thirty minutes or more to get help.

Photo Courtesy of Stephanie Hart

Vaccinations

Even if your Maine Coon is the only pet in the house and lives solely indoors, there are some vaccinations he is required to have. While you may think it unnecessary to vaccinate him for certain illnesses and diseases, all it takes is one slip out the door and into the backyard for your cat to be exposed to a potentially dangerous pathogen or disease.

If you are bringing home a kitten, he may or may not have already had his first round of shots before you pick him up. Be sure to get all medical records and take them with you to the first vet appointment so that you know what he needs and what he has already received. Usually, a kitten will receive his first vaccinations around six to eight weeks and then continue to get vaccinations and boosters in a three- to four-week interval until he is about four months old.

The core vaccinations for cats, as determined by the Feline Vaccination Advisory Panel, include rabies, feline viral rhinotracheitis, calicivirus, panleukopenia (FVRCP), and feline herpesvirus type 1. These are vaccinations recommended for all cats, no matter their lifestyle.

RABIES: Rabies is a very serious viral disease that all mammals are susceptible to, including humans. It is transmitted through the saliva of an infected animal (typically through a bite), and it is usually fatal for an unvaccinated pet. Euthanasia is required by law in several states if rabies is suspected as there is no test to diagnose the disease. The only way to know for sure is to test a postmortem brain sample.

Depending on where you live, several states mandate rabies vaccinations for cats. This shot is typically given first around fourteen to fifteen weeks of age. Some rabies vaccines for cats must be administered yearly, while others last three years. Talk to your vet to know when to schedule your Maine Coon's next rabies vaccine.

FELINE VIRAL RHINOTRACHEITIS/ HERPESVIRUS, CALICIVIRUS, AND PANLEUKOPENIA: Also known as FVRPC, this is a combination vaccine typically administered between six to eight weeks and then again between ten and twelve and fourteen and sixteen weeks. The FVRPC will be administered again at one year and every three years subsequently.

FELINE VIRAL RHINOTRACHEITIS/ HERPESVIRUS: This virus is highly contagious and can potentially affect your Maine Coon for the rest of his life if he encounters it while unvaccinated. Feline herpes causes both respiratory issues and conjunctivitis. While the illness only lasts around ten to twenty days, it will remain dormant in your cat for his entire life and may be reactivated in times of stress or illness.

CALICIVIRUS: This term is used for a broad number of respiratory viruses that this vaccine protects against. Calicivirus also has been shown to cause chronic issues, such as painful inflammation of the gums and teeth.

PANLEUKOPENIA: Panleukopenia, also known as feline parvo, is another highly contagious virus that can quickly turn deadly for a kitten. This virus usually presents with decreased energy and appetite, then progresses to vomiting and diarrhea while killing off white blood cells, making your kitten highly susceptible to secondary infection.

All three of these diseases are highly contagious, found worldwide, and very dangerous for a young kitten. This is why early vaccination is recommended and encouraged.

According to the Feline Vaccination Advisory Panel, there are also some non-core or "lifestyle" vaccinations that you should discuss with your vet to determine if they are right for your Maine Coon. These include the feline leukemia virus, Chlamydophila felis, and Bordetella. Whether or not these shots are recommended will be determined by your own lifestyle factors and environment, so seek advice from a vet that knows you and your cat well.

Parasite Prevention

Parasites such as fleas, ticks, and worms can be an issue even for Maine Coons that live exclusively indoors. One trip out the door is all it takes to pick up one of these pesky critters and all the issues that they bring.

Fleas

Fleas are the most common parasite to afflict cats around the world. They reproduce quickly and are difficult to eradicate once an infestation has taken hold. One single flea can reproduce and lead to an infestation in your home that will be a headache for both you and your cat. Luckily, flea prevention is easy and effective.

TOPICAL FLEA MEDICATION: Topical flea medications for cats are easy and readily available at your local pet stores. This medication comes in a small tube that you squeeze onto your cat's back between the shoulder blades. This medication offers coverage for about one month before it needs to be applied again.

This topical medication works by absorbing into your cat's bloodstream, killing the fleas when they bite. While this medication is effective, it leaves a greasy spot on your cat's fur that should be avoided until it has fully absorbed. Make sure this medication is not in a place accessible for your cat to lick and groom, as he should not ingest the medication.

Most topical flea preventatives have a minimum age, so be sure to consult your vet before beginning. Never use a topical flea medication made for dogs on a cat, as some contain permethrin, which is highly toxic for cats.

ORAL FLEA MEDICATION: Another flea preventative option is an oral medication. Some of these medications even prevent other parasites such as heartworm, mites, and intestinal parasites as well. These medications must be given monthly.

While these are easier and less messy to administer, oral preventatives come with a higher price tag. Not all oral preventatives are created equally, so discuss any medication with your vet before giving it to your Maine Coon.

FLEA COLLARS: Flea collars can be effective against fleas and ticks when used correctly, but they can also be dangerous. Never use a flea collar intended for a dog on a cat as they contain chemicals toxic to your Maine Coon. Be aware that these collars are covered in the same medications you would be administering to your cat through topical application, so care should be taken to avoid all contact with the collar, especially for kids.

How to Treat an Infestation

The last thing a pet owner wants to deal with is a flea infestation. Fleas are very difficult to get rid of, but there are a few things you can do. If your cat has fleas, skip the flea bath. The shampoos used only kill the live fleas on your cat and not the eggs and larvae, meaning they are a temporary solution. Not only do flea shampoos not address the whole problem, but they can actually be harmful to your Maine Coon. Instead, use Dawn dish soap for the exact same result minus the irritation from the medicated shampoo.

You will also need to purchase a flea comb and carefully comb through your cat's fur, all the way down to the skin at a 45-degree angle. These combs are designed with closely spaced teeth that fleas cannot pass between. Comb your entire Maine Coon, but focus on the head, neck, and tail, as this is where fleas love to hide.

If you find a flea in the comb, trap it in a wet paper towel, then drop it in soapy water to kill it. Act quickly, as the fleas move quickly and can jump from the comb once exposed.

Once you have addressed the fleas on your cat, shift the focus to your home, as there may be fleas lurking there as well. Vacuum every area from the floor to the curtains twice a day to ensure the fleas are picked up as they hatch. Empty the vacuum after each time and take the bag outside so any living fleas cannot reenter your home. Do this for two weeks in order to get rid of all the fleas as they hatch. Remember, fleas are rapid reproducers, so don't miss a day.

Ticks

You may think your cat doesn't need tick prevention because he lives primarily indoors, but ticks can find their way inside by several methods, including via humans or other pets. Luckily, most flea preventatives also protect against ticks, but it's important to understand the risks involved with tick bites for your cat.

BOBCAT FEVER: Bobcat fever is the most serious tick-transmitted disease for cats, usually proving fatal just one week after symptoms arise. Transmitted by the Lonestar Tick, bobcat fever is cat-specific and affects a cat's blood cells and circulatory system. Symptoms of bobcat fever include fever, loss of appetite, lethargy, jaundice, and difficulty breathing. While treatment is available, most cats do not survive.

LYME DISEASE: This tick-borne illness is more common in dogs and humans but can sometimes affect cats. Symptoms may include joint stiffness, fever, loss of appetite, sensitivity to touch, and swollen lymph nodes.

ANAPLASMOSIS: A tickborne infection found mainly in the Northeast, symptoms of anaplasmosis include loss of appetite, lethargy, and fever.

Photo Courtesy of Ahli Stevens

Aside from these tick-related illnesses, both fleas and ticks can also cause anemia in your cat if the infestation is large. It is important to check your cat for fleas and ticks regularly, especially after a trip outside or in tall grass or brush. If you do find a tick on your cat, use the following steps to carefully remove it.

1. With gloves, use tweezers to grab the tick firmly and as close to the skin as possible.

2. Once you securely have the tick, pull straight up so that none of the tick's mouthparts are left behind, causing infection.

3. Put the tick in a jar of soapy water to kill it, and clean the tick bite area thoroughly with antiseptic.

4. Keep the tick for identification purposes in the event your cat begins showing symptoms. These may take up to two weeks to present, so watch your Maine Coon closely for changing behavior.

Though both ticks and fleas can be seasonal in many regions, most vets recommend keeping your cat on a year-round preventative.

Worms and Parasites

The most common worms found in cats are hookworms, roundworms, tapeworms, and whipworms. These are fairly common in cats but can be harmful to your cat's health if left untreated. Worms and other internal parasites are typically diagnosed with a stool sample, but there are some symptoms you can keep an eye out for.

Some signs your cat may be infected with a worm or parasite include vomiting, diarrhea, poor skin and coat condition, tar-like stool, weight loss, and a distended abdomen. If you notice any of these symptoms in your cat, even if they are subtle, seek vet care to check your Maine Coon for worms and parasites. If left untreated, symptoms may worsen and even cause death in severe cases.

Heartworms

Most know of the severity of heartworm infestation in dogs, but cats can actually carry these pesky parasites as well. While not common, heartworms can live inside your cat, wreaking havoc on his health. Luckily, the rate of heartworms in cats is low, considering felines are not an ideal host. However, if your cat does happen to become infected, there is no safe and effective treatment for cats like there is for dogs.

These worms are transmitted via mosquito bites and typically take anywhere from six to seven months to develop into adult heartworms, which live in your cat's heart and cause major issues. These worms can cause lung, heart, and artery damage that may be permanent.

Heartworms are common in the southern portion of the United States, especially around the Gulf of Mexico; however, cases have been recorded in all fifty states. Depending on where you live, some vets recommend you protect your cat from heartworms year-round with a preventative, as prevention can mean the difference between life or death for your Maine Coon.

Spay and Neuter

Spaying and neutering are surgical procedures that either remove the uterus and ovaries of a female cat or the testes of the male. If you have purchased your Maine Coon from a breeder, there may be stipulations in your contract that determine if or how quickly you must have these procedures performed.

While some believe you should wait until a cat reaches sexual maturity before spaying or neutering, research has become available showing that there may be more benefits to earlier spay and neutering. If you choose to spay and neuter before sexual maturity is reached, which can be as early as six months, you can avoid some undesirable habits such as spraying, roaming, and aggression. Studies also show that spaying before sexual maturity is reached can also nearly eliminate the risk of mammary tumors or breast cancer for your cat in the future.

Cats can technically be spayed or neutered around the age of eight weeks, and this is typically what shelters and rescues do; however, most owned cats are spayed or neutered just before sexual maturity is reached, between four to six months of age. If your breeder contract doesn't dictate when your cat must be sterilized, discuss the matter with your vet.

Depending on where you live, the cost of a spay or neuter can range from $75-$500, so be prepared to incur that expense before you bring your Maine Coon home. If you are adopting a rescue Maine Coon, he should already be sterilized, and you won't have to worry about the procedure.

Common Genetic Conditions

Although Maine Coon cats are generally considered a healthy breed, there are a few genetic conditions that can plague the breed and cause illness or discomfort. Before you purchase a Maine Coon from a breeder, make sure they have completed all genetic testing needed to prevent passing down any of these genetic conditions.

HYPERTROPHIC CARDIOMYOPATHY (HCM): This is a serious heart condition common to Maine Coons. The genetic mutation that causes HCM can be found in approximately 30 percent of Maine Coons. This mutation causes thickening of the heart walls, which may lead to sudden death or congestive heart failure for your cat.

Symptoms of HCM include lethargy, loss of appetite, difficulty breathing, weak pulse, abnormal heart sounds, inability to exercise, bluish discoloration of the quicks or footpads, sudden hind limb paralysis, crackled breathing, and collapsing. If your Maine Coon exhibits any of these symptoms, seek emergency vet care as soon as possible.

HIP DYSPLASIA: Hip dysplasia occurs when the ball and socket joint connecting the femur to the pelvis does not form correctly. This condition is congenital and cannot be prevented; however, early treatment can slow the progression and make life more comfortable for your cat.

Symptoms of hip dysplasia include pain, limping, resistance to movement, and a changed gait. If you observe any of these changes in your cat, see the vet for an evaluation. Hip dysplasia is diagnosed with an x-ray.

While severe cases may need surgery, most can be managed with pain medication and lifestyle changes. Keeping your cat at an optimal weight is important for improving the quality of life for a Maine Coon with hip dysplasia. Also, reducing strenuous exercises and replacing them with gentle movements can help with pain management. You may need to make things more accessible for your Maine Coon by

HEALTH WATCH
Identifying Hip Dysplasia

Despite being a hardy breed, Maine Coon cats can be more prone to developing breed-specific health issues such as hip dysplasia. Your cat may be suffering from hip dysplasia if you notice limping, difficulty jumping, and lethargy. Progression of hip dysplasia is usually slow and can only be diagnosed by a vet. Treatment varies based on several factors and can include medication, nutritional supplements, and therapy.

placing stools and moveable stairs near the places he loves to access. With proper treatment and care, a Maine Coon can still live a happy and full life with hip dysplasia.

SPINAL MUSCULAR ATROPHY (SMA): SMA is a neurodegenerative disorder that affects the spinal muscles. This condition causes the skeletal muscles of the hind legs to degenerate until the cat has lost almost all use of them. This disease is not fatal or painful for your cat; however, it will require special care for life as it significantly impacts mobility.

SMA typically presents around three to four months of age and progresses fairly quickly, often leaving cats unable to run and jump normally by the age of six months. This disease will not affect your cat's personality or desire to play and be a kitten; however, it will decrease his mobility significantly, making it difficult to do the things he wants to do.

Early signs of spinal muscular atrophy include weakness, tremors in hind legs, odd posture, and a swaying gait. Your cat may also experience back sensitivity and a loss of muscle mass in his hind legs. Because there is no treatment or way to slow the progression of SMA, focus your efforts on keeping your cat happy. Help him access his favorite areas and keep him safely inside, away from predators.

Pet Insurance

Pet insurance is an option for Maine Coons; however, this option needs to be carefully researched. While pet insurance can protect you in the event any conditions arise, it can also be costly and unbeneficial. Each company offers different coverage, so be sure to read the fine print and understand any exclusions; there is almost always an annual deductible you must meet before insurance will cover any costs. Even after that is met, many policies only cover 80 percent, with wellness exams and vaccines not included.

Rates will depend on your cat's age and condition. Unless something considerable comes up, it may be more affordable to simply pay out of pocket for services. Ask your vet what pet insurance he recommends, and go from there.

CHAPTER 11

Traveling with Your Maine Coon

> " *If you want to be able to travel easily with your Maine Coon, make sure to get it used to travel early in kittenhood. Put the cat in a sturdy carrier and take it for frequent short car trips as you do brief errands (make sure to never leave your cat in a hot car!). As it grows, the kitten will understand that this is a normal part of life and will get used to the movement and the sounds. You can take the kitten on overnight trips to pet-friendly hotels, where it can experience different surroundings while still having your comforting company. Find a convenient place in your home to keep the cat carrier in sight and available to the Maine Coon kitten/cat even when it is just hanging out. You will probably find the cat comfortably curled up in it, and there will no longer be the panic of getting the carrier out just for the vet visit. You can also lightly spray the inside of the carrier with cat pheromones to provide a comforting environment.* "
>
> **TERI MATZKIN**
> *SaraJen Maine Coon Cats*

While cats, in general, are natural homebodies, it may be necessary to travel with your cat at times. If you are an avid traveler, however, you may want to reconsider taking on the care of a Maine Coon, as frequent travel can disrupt his routine and cause unneeded stress and anxiety. If you do need to travel with your cat, this chapter will cover all the basics you need to know, as well as helpful tips and tricks to make the experience as easy and painless as possible for both you and your Maine Coon.

*Photo Courtesy
of Liz Holmes
Monster Maine Coons*

Flying with Your Cat

> *If you're flying with your Maine Coon, be sure you have a comfortable carrier that will fit under the seat. Most airlines will have information on the requirements and space available for your cat. It's best not to feed the cat just before leaving, but always have water available. If your cat has travel anxiety, I suggest discussing what options are available with your vet.*
>
> JENNIFER JINKINS
> *Kaiju Maine Coon Cattery*

Depending on the size and weight of your Maine Coon, you may be able to fly with him in the cabin as a carry-on. Typically the weight limit for pets in the cabin is 20 pounds, but every airline's rules and regulations are a little different. Check with your preferred airline before making plans.

Flying with your cat isn't cheap, however, as it can cost anywhere from $100-$125 each way. If your cat is allowed to board the plane with you, he will likely have to remain in an airline-approved carrier under the seat for the entirety of the flight.

Because there are only so many pets allowed on each airplane (this varies by airline and size of the plane), book your flight as early as possible to obtain a spot. In the past, airlines treated cargo animals just like any other luggage. Animals were often left traumatized and sometimes even died because of high or low temperatures, lack of water, etc. Luckily, today, airlines have begun enforcing regulations to keep animals safer on flights.

Not all airlines follow the same guidelines for flying animals. Some require a certificate of veterinary inspection (CVI) and certain vaccines before flying. Make sure you do thorough research on each airline before deciding on the best option for you and your Maine Coon. Federal regulations prohibit any pets under eight weeks old from flying.

Emotional Support Animals

Until a recent FFA rule change, it was possible for your Maine Coon to fly in the cabin with you as long as he was registered as an emotional support cat. This simply required a letter to the airline in advance of the flight. Recent rule changes have deemed that only certified service animals performing a task or benefit for a disabled person will be allowed in the cabin during a flight. This means emotional support animals no longer qualify, and cats are not recognized as official service animals.

Photo Courtesy of Linda Briggs

Hotel Stays

When searching for a hotel to stay in with your Maine Coon, make sure anything you book is pet friendly. It is wise to call ahead and double-check that they allow cats, even if their website says they do, because there is nothing worse than rolling into a hotel only to find out that pets aren't allowed after all. This can save a major headache when you get to the front desk and realize there was a mistake and your cat cannot stay. Checking online for the highest-rated pet-friendly hotels is a great place to start.

Some hotels are known for designating older, outdated, or smoking rooms as pet rooms. Before booking, call and ask if the pet rooms are any different from other rooms so that you know what you are paying for and what to expect. Also, some hotels tack on significant extra fees when staying with a pet, so call ahead to get a good idea of what kind of costs to expect.

Some hotels don't allow pets to be left alone, so make sure you check beforehand if you plan to leave your Maine Coon there for a short time. Always bring a kennel when staying in a hotel, just in case. Even if you don't plan on using the kennel, you never know when something might come up, and you don't want your cat to cause damage in the room if he must be left alone.

VRBO and Air BNB

Other good short-term rental options to explore are Airbnb and VRBO. There are many places that allow pets but also many that do not. When searching for a place to stay, be sure to filter only rentals that allow cats, specifically. Again, it may be smart to call and double-check before booking, just to make sure there is no confusion before you arrive.

Leaving Your Cat Behind

After evaluating the cost and potential stress involved with traveling with your Maine Coon, you may want to explore options for leaving him behind as well. There are several options when it comes to cat care while you are away from home.

Cat Sitters

If you're not planning to be away for an extended period of time, it may be beneficial for your Maine Coon to simply stay home. Hiring a cat sitter to check on your cat regularly can ease his stress while you are away by allowing him to stay in a comfortable and familiar environment. Find a pet-sitter through online resources such as petsitter.com or ask a responsible family member or friend to come and take care of your cat.

Because cats are pretty self-sufficient, they won't need much more than to be fed and watered, given some attention, and to have their litter box cleaned periodically. If you feel more comfortable, you can also hire a 24-hour cat sitter to stay overnight with your cat. Of course, this is a much more expensive care option.

HELPFUL TIP
Car Safety

While all cats are different, most cats can be persuaded to enjoy car travel with early socialization and training. Starting small with short trips or even spending time together in a parked car are great ways to acclimate your cat to car travel. Using a cat carrier, either secured to the back seat or in the trunk, away from the airbags, is the safest option for car travel with your Maine Coon. Be sure to bring food and water as well as a harness and leash. Puppy pads are good insurance against bathroom accidents or carsickness as well. Maine Coons are extremely intelligent and can make excellent travel companions with time and patience.

Boarding

If you don't feel comfortable leaving your cat alone, you may choose to board your cat at a full-care facility. This is a place where you take your cat and drop him off to stay until you are ready to pick him back up. Do your research before choosing a place, and make sure to read reviews on how they handle cats. Also, it is not wise to take your cat to a boarder unless he is up to date on any and all vaccines he may need beforehand.

Some cat boarders will offer suite services allowing your cat to roam free in a private suite full of cat-friendly toys. However, not all places offer this, and some simply kennel cats much like they would at a veterinary office, so it's important you ask ahead about the accommodations.

Rates for boarding facilities typically range between $25-$35 a night and include a range of amenities. If you are worried about leaving your Maine Coon behind, look for a facility that provides a streaming service so you can check in on your cat anytime you want.

Whichever route you choose, make sure you are confident and comfortable with the choice so that you can rest easy while you are away. The last thing you want on a trip is to be consumed with worry about your loving Maine Coon.

More Tips and Tricks for Traveling

> "
>
> *Do not feed cats prior to travel to lessen motion sickness. Don't place the crate near the back of the vehicle to lessen the incidence of motion sickness. Cover the travel crate or carrier so that the cat cannot see objects such as trees moving by quickly to prevent motion sickness. Always place cats in a crate to keep them from getting under the gas or brake pedals, or from jumping out whenever someone opens the door.*
>
> KELLY SPARKMAN
> *Mountain Fork European Maine Coons*
>
> "

No matter how far you are going, whether it's down the street or across the country, use these tips to help any trip with your Maine Coon be as stress-free as possible.

- Don't feed your cat within four hours of any trip. This includes car rides, plane rides, and any other method of transportation. This may help prevent your having to clean up vomit or excess drool, as cats are prone to carsickness.

- Don't sedate your cat! This once common practice is no longer recommended by veterinarians. Sedating a cat can inhibit his ability to react in an emergency and is not good for his health.

- Travel with a harness and lead, and be sure to practice with it at home if your Maine Coon isn't accustomed to it.

- Check-in as late as possible at the airport so that your cat doesn't have to spend the extra time waiting in his carrier.

- If you are flying, make sure that your rental car or car service allows for pets to ride.

- Always have a bowl, food, and water with you. No matter how you are traveling, these basic items will be necessities, especially in case of an emergency. Also, keep a litter box and fresh litter handy for potty breaks on very long trips.

- If you're driving, use a kennel to keep your cat safely confined and as comfortable as possible. Never let him roam the car free, as he could become a distraction and cause an accident.

- Always have the number of a local emergency vet on hand. Emergencies can happen anywhere, so look up local animal hospitals before you travel—just in case.

CHAPTER 12

Into the World of Showing

The Maine Coon cat makes a perfect companion pet. However, some owners decide to delve into the world of cat shows with this beautiful breed as well. If you're thinking about purchasing a show-quality Maine Coon or will be entering your cat into a show, this chapter will give you all the information you need.

All About Cat Shows

A cat show is an event where cats of all different breeds are brought together and judged based on appearance, structure, and characteristics based on that breed's standards. Cat shows have been taking place for centuries in Europe. However, the first prominent cat show in the United States took place in New York City's Madison Square Garden in 1895. Unlike dog shows, which most people are relatively familiar with, the cats are not paraded around on leashes and walked in a circle. Instead, they are placed in individual cages behind a table of judges.

Typically, each judge will take a cat out of the cage, examine it for judging, and then place the cat back into its designated cage. Depending on the show, owners may be allowed to stay and watch the judging if the show is "open style," or they may be asked to leave the hall if it is "closed style."

Cat show season begins in May and runs through April, with shows often being multi-day events. These shows can draw large crowds of thousands and hundreds of cats. With all cat shows sponsored by breed registries, the best-known shows are held by the Cat Fanciers Association, the International Cat Association, and the American Cat Fanciers Association.

Classes

Each show sponsor uses a different classification system for judging. Shows held by the **CAT FANCIERS ASSOCIATION** place cats into one of seven categories. They include the following:

Championship: These entries are unaltered pedigreed cats.

Premiership: These cats are pedigreed but altered.

Veteran: These are pedigreed cats that are above the age of seven.

Household Pet: These are non-pedigreed cats of any kind.

Provisional: These are breeds that are partially but not fully recognized by the association.

Miscellaneous: These breeds are not recognized by the association.

Kitten: These entries are pedigreed kittens between the ages of four and eight months.

In contrast, the **INTERNATIONAL CAT ASSOCIATION** uses only three classifications:

Championship: These entries include pedigreed kittens and adults, unaltered or altered.

Household Pets: These are unpedigreed kittens or adult cats.

New Breed or Color: These are pedigreed kittens or adults of a new breed or color.

Shows hosted by the **AMERICAN CAT FANCIERS ASSOCIATION** are placed into one of five categories.

Kittens: These are kittens between the ages of four and eight months with a pedigree.

New Breed or Color: These entries are pedigreed cats whose breed or color isn't yet recognized for the championship division.

Championship: These cats are pedigreed and unaltered.

Alters: These cats are pedigreed but have been altered.

Household Pets: These are non-pedigreed and mixed-breed cats.

Whether or not your Maine coon has an official pedigree will determine which class he will be placed in. If he is pedigreed and placed into championship class or an altered class, he will be judged by Maine Coon breed standards. If he is not officially pedigreed, he will be judged in the household pets class and will not be held to the Maine Coon breed standard. Instead, he will be judged on overall appearance, physical condition, playfulness, and personality. For more information and a detailed description of the Maine Coon breed standard, see chapter 1.

Should I Enter My Cat?

Unless you bought your Maine Coon specifically to show, you may be asking yourself whether or not your cat is ready to enter a show. Typically, any aggressive behavior by a scared cat will land you with a disqualification, so it's important you don't throw your cat into the ring without proper

DID YOU KNOW?
Colorful Cats

Maine Coon cats come in 75 different colors, from solid to tabby, tortoiseshell, blue, or black! The rarest colors for Maine Coons are shaded silver and golden. A shaded silver Maine Coon has pale fur at the root and darker gray at the tips. Golden Maine Coons have hair with orange roots and black tips. Solid orange Maine Coons can also be difficult to find, while black Maine Coons are the most common.

preparation. Before considering entry for your beautiful Maine Coon, attend a few cat shows as a spectator to get a feel for the atmosphere. This will help you better determine if your cat would be able to handle the setting.

Grooming is an important part of cat shows, so if your Maine Coon is reluctant to sit through a grooming session, he may not be ready for a show yet. Since most shows require a cat's claws be trimmed, that is something you need to practice and get your cat accustomed to before committing to a cat show.

A cat show will also require your Maine Coon to be held in a cage for a period of time without you present, so if your cat becomes fearful in new spaces or around other cats, he probably isn't ready for a cat show.

How to Enter a Cat Show

If your Maine Coon is ready to enter his first show, it is time to complete your official show entry form. Show entry forms are typically available online, or you can request a paper version instead. Be prepared with all of your cat's information, including his name, registration number, date of birth, sex, eye color, color class number, breed, color descriptions, sire and dam name, breeder, owner name, and your own personal information. You will also need to know what class to select for your cat, so refer to the list above for that information.

Many shows also offer special requests on their entry forms, which will require additional fees. These special requests include grooming spaces for before the show, end-of-row cage spots, or specific placement next to another cat. You can also request a double cage, which may be advised for a large breed such as the Maine Coon. Once your entry form is complete, you can send it in via post, fax, or through the online entry method of that particular show.

Photo Courtesy
of Stephanie Hart

The Cost of Showing

Every cat show will have an entry fee that helps the club pay for the cost of hosting the event. These fees vary from show to show, so check with your particular show. Aside from the entry fees, take into account the additional fees you may incur, such as requesting a double cage, a grooming space, or any other special requests you may have.

Not only will the show itself have fees, but consider the cost of travel, an overnight stay if needed, food costs, and anything else you may need while at the show. Time spent preparing for the show should also be a consideration. Many owners spend hours grooming before a show, not to mention the time spent preparing their cat to be handled in the show ring. It can be both labor-intensive and time-consuming.

Preparing for the Show

When heading to a cat show, make sure you bring all the supplies you and your cat will need. These items include food, water, bowls, a litter box, toys to keep your Maine Coon entertained, and any grooming tools you need. It is also wise to bring current vet records and vaccination documentation, just in case there are any questions.

You will also need to provide a curtain for your cat's cage. This is simply a visual barrier put up between cages so that cats do not interact with each other. This can be something as simple as a towel, or it can be an opportunity to showcase your cat and his appearance. Many people choose to go all out with their curtains and pick a color that complements their cat's coat or eye color. These curtains can become pretty extravagant.

Arrive at the show hall at least one to two hours before judging begins. When you get there, you will need to check in with the entry clerk and get your cage number. Find your cage right away to avoid any confusion as judging time approaches. Familiarize yourself with the event center and locate each ring well in advance.

If you are paying for a grooming space, you will want to arrive at the event center and claim your space with enough time to complete any final grooming of your cat.

Awards

As the show begins, a judge will preside over each ring or group of cats and award them accordingly. There are typically several rings in each show. Cats compete for rosettes and points, which accumulate over a season to be tallied at the end. There are no cash prizes won at cat shows. Some of the many titles available to win are the following:

- First, second, and third place
- Best and second-best in color
- Best and second in best of breed
- Best long-haired championship
- Best short-haired championship
- Household pet merit award
- Best cat
- Best kitten

Each association will tally points and merits at the end of the season and recognize the most accomplished cats. They will also announce the top regional winners for each area.

While cat shows can be fun and exciting for both a Maine Coon enthusiast and an outgoing Maine Coon, it's important to determine what is right for your cat before jumping into the show world. Not all cats will tolerate the atmosphere or enjoy the pace of a cat show, so be sure to take your feline friend's lead. If you try one show and it seems to cause your cat stress, it may be best to become a spectator rather than a competitor.

CHAPTER 13

Your Aging Maine Coon Cat

With a life span of about twelve to fifteen years, a Maine Coon reaches senior status around the age of eleven. Just as humans do, your Maine Coon's health will likely decline gradually as he ages and grows into his senior years. No matter how your cat's health evolves in his later years, this chapter will help you walk through those changes together, making the needed adjustments so that he can live a healthy, full life for the rest of his days.

Common Old-Age Ailments

> *As your Maine Coon ages, you should have your veterinarian check the cat for hip dysplasia. Maine Coons are predisposed to this issue. Senior cats should also be fed a low phosphorus food. Glucosamine supplements can help support an aging cat's joints. If your cat starts to have trouble using the litter box, visit your veterinarian to rule out any health issues. The cat may need a litter box that is easier for it to get in and out of or closer to where it usually hangs out. As your Maine Coon ages, continue to feed it quality food, play with it, and give it lots of love. Senior cats deserve the same amount of attention as when they were kittens. Old cats still love to play; they just move a little bit slower.*
>
> CORIE AND MATTHEW HELMS
> *Rocketmans Maine Coons*

RENAL DISEASE: Chronic kidney disease is common in elderly cats. As your Maine Coon ages, his kidneys can become less effective, filtering less

Photo Courtesy
of Liz Holmes
Monster Maine Coons

of the waste and toxins from his bloodstream, allowing it to build up to unhealthy levels. This buildup is known as azotemia.

Because chronic kidney disease often goes unnoticed until about 75% of kidney function is lost, it's very important to screen your Maine Coon at his regular vet checkups, even if you aren't noticing any symptoms.

Symptoms of chronic renal disease include increased thirst, decreased appetite, weight loss, vomiting, lethargy, bloody or cloudy urine or a change in urine frequency, bad breath, and poor coat quality. If you notice any of these symptoms in your Maine Coon, have him checked by a vet as soon as possible. The quicker you catch chronic renal failure, the more time you have to address the cause and make changes to slow the progression.

ARTHRITIS: Although it often goes undiagnosed due to a cat's natural survival instinct to hide pain and discomfort, arthritis is not uncommon in aging Maine Coons. Have your vet check for sore or painful joints at each of his appointments. If there is any sign of pain or discomfort, an X-ray may be needed to confirm the diagnosis.

Some signs your cat may be dealing with arthritis are a general reduction in activity, a reluctance to jump, jumping shorter or lower distances than is typical, difficulty using the litter box, sleeping in lower, easier-to-access places, changes in his grooming routine, and irritability. If you notice any of these symptoms in your Maine Coon, have him checked out by a vet in a timely manner.

Arthritis is not a death sentence for your Maine Coon, but it does mean changes need to be made. Depending on the severity of the arthritis, your vet may prescribe nonsteroidal anti-inflammatory drugs for pain management, dietary supplements, and lifestyle changes. Discuss treatment options with your vet to keep your cat happy and comfortable.

There are several dietary supplements available for arthritis support in cats. These typically contain some combination of glycosaminoglycans, such as glucosamine and chondroitin, which can help improve cartilage condition, and essential fatty acids, which can help reduce inflammation. Never give your cat a supplement without consulting your vet first.

Although supplements can provide supportive care, they are not regulated, and quality can vary greatly from product to product. Be sure to do your research to find a quality supplement and ask your vet for recommendations.

Some cat owners have also sought alternative care for their cat's arthritis by utilizing acupuncture. While there are no conclusive studies showing the effectiveness of acupuncture, anecdotal evidence supports the use of this alternative therapy in addition to other treatments.

When dealing with arthritis, basic lifestyle changes are often needed to keep your cat comfortable and ease his stress. These lifestyle changes may include things like lowering his food and water to a location that is easier to access, keeping all his things on the ground level of the house, switching to a low-sided litter box for easy entry, and providing ramps to his favorite elevated spaces. Obesity is another factor that can worsen arthritis, so speak to your vet about weight management if you suspect your Maine Coon is overweight.

HYPERTHYROIDISM: As your Maine Coon ages, his thyroid function may decline and cause a host of issues. Hyperthyroidism is not uncommon in aging cats and is caused by an overproduction of the thyroid hormone. Symptoms of hyperthyroidism can be shedding more than usual, weight loss, excess thirst and hunger, and overactivity. If your cat is diagnosed with hyperthyroidism, your vet will likely prescribe daily medication to regulate his hormone levels.

DID YOU KNOW?
World's Longest Cat

The Guinness World Record for the longest cat ever belongs to a Maine Coon named Mymains Stewart Gilligan, a.k.a. Stewie, who measured 123 centimeters long. Stewie lived in Reno, Nevada, with his owners Robin Hendrickson and Erik Brandsness. This impressively long Maine Coon set the record on August 28, 2010. Unfortunately, he passed away in January 2013. The current longest cat alive is a Maine Coon named Ludo who lives in Wakefield, UK. Ludo measures 118.33 centimeters long.

FELINE LYMPHOMA: Lymphoma is the most common cancer in cats and is commonly found in the intestines. Symptoms of lymphoma include weight loss, lethargy, poor appetite, vomiting, and diarrhea. While feline lymphoma is more common in older cats, it's important to note that it can occur at any time in a Maine Coon's life.

Treatment for feline lymphoma depends greatly on how quickly it is diagnosed and what stage it is. Chemotherapy, steroids, and surgery are all possible treatment options for a cat with this disease. The quicker lymphoma is detected, the better the chance for longer survival, so it's very important to keep up with your aging cat's vet checkups and relay any changes you notice as soon as possible.

DIABETES: Aging cats are susceptible to diabetes, just as humans are. Symptoms to watch out for are increased urination, increased thirst, increased appetite, and weight loss. Have your cat checked by a vet immediately if he is exhibiting any of these symptoms.

Treatment for feline diabetes may include glucose monitoring and insulin injections. Your vet will likely recommend diet and lifestyle changes as well to help promote good health and possible remission of symptoms.

DENTAL DISEASE: Without consistent dental care throughout a cat's life, a buildup of tartar and plaque can cause painful dental diseases as your Maine Coon ages. The two most common are periodontal disease, which is progressive and painful swelling and inflammation of the gums, and tooth resorption, which is a progressive deterioration of the tooth.

Though cats typically hide their pain and discomfort, some signs and symptoms of dental disease are increased food pickiness, such as a preference for wet or soft foods, gum bleeding, head shaking, and pawing at the mouth.

The best prevention for dental disease as your Maine Coon ages is consistent dental care throughout his life. Talk to your vet about teeth cleanings and brush your cat's teeth daily, beginning when he is a kitten to get him used to it.

OBESITY: As your Maine Coon ages into his senior years, his activity level will naturally begin to decline. This can cause weight gain, which can put your cat more at risk for some of these previously mentioned age-related conditions. If you notice your cat gaining weight, discuss weight management options with the vet. He may recommend a special diet or an increase in activity.

Other Common Senior Cat Issues

As your cat ages, his body will naturally decline in ways that may alter his life. These include deafness, sight problems or blindness, incontinence, and even dementia. These common issues are to be expected as a cat grows into his older years, just as they are with humans. While these aren't always problems that will shorten his life, you will need to make major adjustments in the home to keep him safe and able to function as independently as possible.

DEAFNESS: Some signs your cat's hearing may be in decline are sudden disobedience, not responding to his name or other noises, and pawing at his ears. If you notice any of these symptoms, there are some things you can do to prepare him for possible further hearing loss.

For example, begin calling for his attention at the same time you flash a flashlight or a laser pointer in front of him. This can help him associate the sight with the sound of you wanting his attention. Eventually, if he loses his hearing altogether, he will already be trained to give you attention with the light flashes. Some cats may also be attuned to vibrations, and a moderate tap on the floor or table may garner his attention.

If your cat loses his hearing, consider keeping him inside and taking him out on leashed walks instead. A deaf cat cannot hear approaching danger and may not be aware of oncoming traffic or predators while he is out and about.

Photo Courtesy
of Ahli Stevens

BLINDNESS: A decline in sight in your cat may be evident by symptoms such as disorientation, bumping into things, and startling easily. If you notice your Maine Coon exhibiting any of these signs, see a vet right away.

If a visual decline is inevitable for your cat, there are a few things you can do to keep him comfortable and happy. First, as his vision declines, he will likely startle easily as he cannot see like he used to. Be sure to set him at ease every time you approach by giving friendly verbal cues that you are near.

It is also important that you do not move things around the house. Leaving things where they are will help him from becoming disoriented and bumping into things that are in a new place. Do not pick your blind cat up and carry him everywhere. Instead, allow him to navigate his way so he can remain independent.

A blind cat should have all the things he needs on the ground level. Placing your cat on an elevated surface is dangerous as he could easily fall off.

INCONTINENCE: Though it isn't fun to think about, incontinence is something that can happen to any aging cat. If your cat suddenly seems to lose control over his bladder, seek vet care as there may be a helpful treatment available.

For cats that become incontinent due to loss of muscle control, a muscle stimulant may be prescribed to help them gain back some of that function. Also, be sure to have an easily accessible, low-sided litter box so that he isn't discouraged from using it.

If your cat is struggling with incontinence, and nothing seems to be helping, diapers are an option but should be used with caution. Trapping urine and feces in a diaper promotes sores and rashes on your cat's skin so he will need to be thoroughly cleaned and changed frequently.

MENTAL AWARENESS: The mental clarity of your Maine Coon may also decline in his senior years. Cat dementia, also known as feline cognitive dysfunction, is an age-related decline in cognitive clarity and function. If you notice disorientation, changes in behavior such as sleep patterns, confusion, or even unusual vocal sounds, have your Maine Coon checked out by a vet.

While age-related dementia is not reversible, there are ways to possibly slow down the progression. Keep your cat stimulated and exercise his brain regularly with games such as laser pointer activities, feathers, and other enriching stimuli. This can help him stay sharp and mentally aware.

Basic Senior Cat Care

As previously mentioned, a senior cat should see the vet twice a year for checkups. Even if your cat is not afflicted with any typically age-related illnesses, he will still need some lifestyle adjustments to accommodate his aging body.

Grooming

As your Maine Coon ages, he may find it more difficult to efficiently groom himself like he used to. Older cats may need more assistance keeping their coats clean and free of matting. For a cat with a long coat like the Maine Coon, daily brushing is recommended as he ages to help keep his coat in tip-top shape.

Because your senior cat's joints will be more sensitive, use a very gentle touch while grooming your older cat and consider switching to a soft-bristle brush that isn't too hard on his skin and joints. Be sure to make the daily grooming session a positive experience with plenty of pets and verbal praise, and your aging cat will likely grow to love all the additional attention.

His coat isn't the only thing he may have difficulty maintaining himself. An aging Maine Coon may also find it more difficult to keep his claws filed down just by scratching. If he seems less willing to use an upright scratching post, try switching to one that is lower to the ground. If your cat still isn't filing his claws like he used to, you may need to trim the claws for him. See chapter 9 for a detailed description of how to do that.

> **"**
>
> *As your cat ages, its dietary needs change, and with today's pet foods, we can adjust food to cats' age-related needs. Cats may need softer food if their teeth are starting to be an issue. As cats get older, they tend to groom themselves less, so they need a bit more care in that area. If the cat is getting thin, check with your vet to make sure there isn't a health issue other than age going on. Know that, just like people, senior cats are going to slow down and have some aches and pains. Make sure they are able to get to the litter and food and have a place to sleep in a sunny spot. They may start to need a bit more help getting up on things and may move a bit slower. If you notice something that seems wrong, get your senior cat checked by the vet.*
>
> WENDY MEYER
> *Theatricats*
>
> **"**

Illness and Injury Prevention

Just as human bodies do, your Maine Coon's body will decline as he gets into his senior years. This means he will be more prone to accident, injury, and illness. This is a normal progression of life; however, there are some things you can do to prevent illness and injury as best you can.

As well as taking your cat to the vet for his twice-yearly checkups, you can also discuss vaccines with your vet to make sure your Maine Coon is fully up to date on everything he may need. Illness takes a much greater toll on an elderly cat, so it's important to keep him up to date as a preventative measure.

When you begin to see a physical decline in your aging Maine Coon, it's time to make the lifestyle changes that can help prevent serious injury. This may be lowering his food, keeping his favorite things on the ground level, and investing in ramps to help him access his favorite spots. These may seem like small changes, but they can prevent an aging cat from jumping from a place too high and injuring himself.

Even as you see his physical capabilities wane, it's important that you keep your aging cat active, as this can also help prevent injury. Engage your Maine Coon in some gentle play and get him moving in a safe way. This can also help keep his weight down, further preventing other age-related illness and disease.

If your aging Maine Coon is dealing with arthritis or simply seems slower moving than he was in his younger years, consider getting him an orthopedic bed to sleep on. These foam beds are designed to relieve pressure and provide your cat with a comfortable rest. Since he can spend up to twenty hours a day sleeping, a comfortable place for old joints to rest is important.

If your senior Maine Coon has a difficult time regulating his body temperature, a self-warming cat bed may be just the luxury the vet ordered. These beds are electric and can help entice a cold cat to snuggle up and warm himself on a cold day. Be sure to use with caution as a curious cat may be enticed by the connected wire. Use a heated bed only when you are home to monitor.

> "
> Cats have the ultimate ability of hiding any pain or discomfort. You need to be diligent about changes in your cat's behavior. Regular vet visits with blood work are an invaluable source of info on the health of your cat. Keep your cat a healthy weight and indoors, and your cat should live many, many years.
>
> DEBORAH KINSLEY
> *Tufts N Trills Maine Coons*
> "

Supplements and Nutrition

Some Maine Coon owners turn to supplements to keep their aging cat healthy and agile. Unfortunately, most supplements are unregulated and have not been tested in cats to determine whether or not they are safe for use. If you want to provide your Maine Coon with an additional vitamin supplement or glucosamine for joint support, discuss this with your vet beforehand and use only what he is willing to recommend.

Never assume that a supplement safe for a dog is safe for a cat. There are many supplements and herbal treatments approved for dogs that are untested or even toxic to cats.

The best way to provide your senior Maine Coon with all the nutrients he needs to thrive is to feed him a quality, well-balanced diet. If your Maine Coon is less willing to eat a dry kibble at mealtimes, try mixing it with wet food. Not only can wet food be easier on aging teeth, but it can also help him stay hydrated, which is imperative to proper kidney function.

As your cat ages, his nutritional needs may change. As his body physically declines, he may need fewer calories to maintain a healthy body mass. While the Association of American Feed Control Officials has made no distinction between adult and senior cat foods requirements, you should consult your vet to know if and when you may need to switch his food. As long as your Maine Coon is maintaining his health and a healthy body weight, there is no need to switch foods simply because he is aging. However, if he is gaining weight due to becoming less physically active or a natural decline of metabolism, a change may be in order.

If you and your vet decide to change your cat's food, make sure you transition him over a period of several days. An abrupt diet change can cause your cat gastrointestinal upset, or he may simply refuse to eat something he isn't used to. Instead, begin the transition by feeding him three-quarters of his old food with one-quarter of the new. If he tolerates that well, try half and half the next day. On day three, give him three-quarters of the new food with one-quarter of the old. Finally, by day four, he should be ready for a complete meal with the new food.

If your Maine Coon doesn't adjust that quickly to the new food, transition him more gradually over a longer period of time. If your senior cat refuses to eat or becomes unusually finicky, have him checked out by the vet for any health issues. Remember, cats are masters at hiding their pain and discomfort. Finicky eating may be nothing, but it could be a subtle sign that something isn't right.

CHAPTER 14

When It's Time to Say Goodbye

Though the thought seems unbearable, there comes a time in every Maine Coon owner's life when the realization that the cat's pain outweighs his joy becomes undeniable. When this time comes, it's important to remember that it's our duty to our beloved feline friend to thank him for the years of love he gave and end his suffering humanely. Undoubtedly, this is one of the most difficult parts of being a Maine Coon owner.

Many people believe that it is one of the toughest and greatest responsibilities of animal ownership to know when to humanely relieve an animal from pain when the end of life is inevitable. It is never an easy decision and often leads to an array of emotions for the owner, including sorrow, guilt, and second thoughts.

The Tough Decision

You may be wondering how you can possibly know when the time is right to say goodbye. Unfortunately, there is no clear answer to that question. Your cat may have good days and bad days, but no one knows your Maine Coon better than you, and nobody will be able to make this decision for you. The bond you and your cat share is unlike any other, and that is exactly what makes you the right person to make the final call.

A Sharp Decline

If you have a gut feeling your senior cat is making a sharp decline and suffering more pain than joy, it may be time to say goodbye. A few telltale signs that death is imminent are loss of coordination, incontinence, extreme lack of interest in anything, seeking solitude, and not eating or drinking anything.

Only you and your Maine Coon will truly know when this time comes. Your cat has been your loving companion for years, trusting you with his life. He trusts you with it now as well. If you believe death is imminent and that humanely putting the cat down will end his suffering, speak to your vet about euthanasia.

Once you and your vet agree that death is inevitable, the process happens fairly quickly. The point is to end your cat's suffering, so there isn't any point in putting it off.

The Euthanasia Process

Before you take your Maine Coon to the vet, call any friends or family members who may want to say goodbye. Some vets also offer to come to your home and perform euthanasia there in order to make the process easier for your cat. Either way, you will have the option to be present when the vet performs the procedure. Although it may be hard for you to watch your Maine Coon die, know that it will bring your cat comfort and peace in his last moments if you are there with him, holding him and comforting him.

Photo Courtesy of Victoria Wassell

During the procedure, your vet will administer a solution, typically phenobarbital, intravenously. The solution is usually thick with a blue, pink, or purple tint. The vet may inject it directly into a vein or into an intravenous catheter. Once the solution is injected, it will quickly travel through your cat's body, causing him to lose consciousness within just a few seconds. Your Maine Coon will feel no pain. Breathing will slow and then stop completely, followed by cardiac arrest, which will cause death, typically within thirty seconds of the injection.

When death seems apparent, your vet will check for signs of life and then will most likely step out of the room to give you a chance to say a final goodbye. Your cat's body may still move after death, so don't be alarmed if you see twitching. He may also release bodily fluids, and this is also normal.

Your vet and his office staff have been through this before and will understand the emotional weight of the situation for you. They should provide you with privacy and be a source of comfort if needed. Be sure to make payments and after-death arrangements beforehand so that you don't have to deal with it after.

Final Arrangements

Cremation is a common option for those who want to memorialize their beloved Maine Coon. It is more economical than finding a plot in a pet cemetery, and it's a relatively simple process. If you have chosen to have your cat cremated, your vet will coordinate with a funeral home or cremation service and notify you when your pet's ashes are ready.

If you are taking your deceased cat home for burial, the vet will place your cat's remains in a container and will typically carry it out to the car for you. Though burying your pet at home is legal in most states, it may not be the best idea. When burying a pet at home, be aware that your cat's remains could resurface due to a flood, be dug up by a wild animal, or even contaminate the soil and groundwater with dangerous bacteria. If you choose to have a memorial at your home, consider spreading your cat's ashes there instead of a burial.

DID YOU KNOW?
The Oldest Maine Coon

A Maine Coon cat named Corduroy was named Oldest Living Cat by Guinness World Records at 26 years old in 2015. Corduroy lived in Oregon with his owner, Ashley Okura, who adopted him as a kitten in 1989. Maine Coon cats live an average of 12 to 15 years. Corduroy's brother, Batman, lived an impressive 19 years.

A pet cemetery is another option for a final resting place for your Maine Coon. This is a designated graveyard for pets to be buried safely. This service is pricey and costs around 400– 600 dollars just for the plot. Casket prices vary in addition to those fees. While it is an expensive option, your Maine Coon will rest in a beautiful area among other loved pets.

Whichever you choose, once you leave the vet's office, you will begin the grieving process. Hold on to the love and memories you share, and your loving Maine Coon will never be forgotten.

Grieving the Loss

The loss of a beloved pet is never easy and often hurts like the loss of a family member. Remember that it's completely okay to seek the help of a counselor or therapist to help you through this difficult time. Make sure you don't rush the grief and allow yourself to honor the memory of your Maine Coon companion. The time you spent together will always be etched into your heart.

Made in the USA
Columbia, SC
14 September 2023

22876617R00070